PRACTICAL
EGYPTIAN
MAGIC

By the same author
PRACTICAL TECHNIQUES OF PSYCHIC SELF-
   DEFENSE
THE WAY OF CARTOUCHE

PRACTICAL EGYPTIAN MAGIC

Murry Hope

St. Martin's Griffin
New York

Library of Congress Cataloging in Publication Data

Hope, Murry.
    Practical Egyptian magic.

    Bibliography: p.
    Includes index.
    1. Magic, Egyptian.   I. Title.
BF1591.H63 1986   133.4′3   86-1276
ISBN 0-312-63474-9

First published in Great Britain by Aquarian Press, Thorsons Publishing Group.

10 9 8 7

ACKNOWLEDGEMENTS

Grateful appreciation to Cyril Aldred and his publishers, Thames and Hudson, for permitting use of the chronological tables from *The Egyptians*; and to artist Martin Jones for his excellent illustrations of Egyptian symbols.

Murry Hope
June 1983

CONTENTS

PREFACE

The ensuing work presupposes a fair knowledge of occult semantics and at least some degree of familiarity with the metaphysical world. As the word 'magic' itself tends to have controversial overtones for the uninitiated – there still being people who associate it either with what are ignorantly referred to as the 'black arts' or with entertainers who produce objects from hats by sleight of hand – a clear definition is necessary.

I could not hope to put it better than the late A.E. Waite. In his book, *The Occult Sciences*, he writes:

> The popular conception of Magic, even when it is not identified with the trickeries of imposture and the pranks of the mountebank, is entirely absurd and gross.
>
> 'Magic, or, more accurately, Magism,' says Christian in his *Histoire de la Magie*, 'if anyone would condescend to return to its antique origin, could be no longer confounded with the superstitions which calumniate its memory. Its name is derived to us from the Greek words MAGOS, a Magician, and MAGELA, Magic, which are merely permutations of the terms MOG, MEGH, MAGH, which in Pehlvi and in Zend, both languages of the eldest East, signify "priest", "wise" and "excellent". It was thence also that, in a period anterior to historic Greece, there originated the Chaldean name Maghdim, which is equivalent to "supreme wisdom", or sacred philosophy. Thus, mere etymology indicates that Magic was the synthesis of those sciences once possessed by the Magi or philosophers

of India, of Persia, of Chaldea, and of Egypt, who were the priests of nature, the patriarchs of knowledge, and the founders of those vast civilizations whose ruins still maintain, without tottering, the burden of sixty centuries.'

Ennemoser, in his *History of Magic* (as translated by Howitt), says 'Among the Parsees, the Medes and the Egyptians, a higher knowledge of nature was understood by the term Magic, with which religion, and particularly astronomy, were associated. The initiated and their disciples were called Magicians – that is, the Wise – which was also the case among the Greeks . . . Plato understood by Wisdom nothing less than a worship of the Divinity, and Apuleius says that Magus means, in the Persian language, a priest . . . India, Persia, Chaldea and Egypt, were the cradles of the oldest Magic. Zoroaster, Ostanes, the Brahmins, the Chaldean sages, and the Egyptian priests, were the primitive possessors of its secrets. The priestly and sacrificial functions, the healing of the sick, and the preservation of the Secret Wisdom, were the objects of their life. They were either princes themselves, or surrounded princes as their counsellors. Justice, truth, and the power of self-sacrifice, were the great qualities with which each one of these must be endowed; and the neglect of any one of these virtues was punished in the most cruel manner.'

This scholarly and erudite apology continues for several more pages, but the essence of its message is the same throughout and applies even more so today than when it was first published in 1891.

M.H.

INTRODUCTION

It has been suggested in recent years, by both scientists and mystics, that time is neither linear nor movable but exists in stationary bands through which we, as individual minds or incarnate essences, move in order to gain experience. On this premise we can adjust our attitude towards what is broadly referred to as 'ancient Egypt' and consider those time-shrouded days to be as close to us now as more recent and better documented epochs. The Aquarian Age, we are taught, is a time to return to simple, natural truths; a time to discard the multiple layers of accumulated veneer that have resulted from centuries of religious and political oppression; a time for the individual to seek his true identity through his basic cosmic roots.

Egypt and its magical past has much to contribute towards a better and broader understanding of our cosmic origins and our future inter-cosmic connections. It completes a circle, as it were, a circle in time that closes the yawning gap between pure faith in the existence of external forces and a practical knowledge of, and communication with, those forces that could enrich the quality of life for many and make a valid contribution towards easing the stresses brought about by the slow and painful transition from Piscean to Aquarian principles and life standards.

Before we can make that journey of discovery into Egypt's dim and distant past, it is necessary to strip away some of the overlays and substructures that have presented themselves in different guises over the three thousand or more years that spanned that country's early history. When the subject of Egyptology is raised one so often hears the same remarks or rejoinders: 'Oh, yes, that's King Tut's tomb and all that; didn't they worship cats or crocodiles and mummify everything in sight?' In fact, religious and magical beliefs in, say, the much popularized eighteenth dynasty, when Akhnaton introduced his Aten icon at Amarna and King Tut was buried in all splendour, were quite different from those adhered to in the first dynasty, or in the later times so vividly described by Herodotus. And yet, in spite of the many cultural and sub-cultural superimpositions, a thread of magical truth has survived the ravages of the centuries and found its way into the teachings and beliefs of present day occultists and mystics. Nor have the basic principles of Egyptian magic ever ceased to be relevant to man and his life, which is because they were learned from an even older and wiser peoples who based them on inter-cosmic principles that, like cosmic law, are constant in all spheres of existence throughout the universe.

To facilitate a broader understanding of the enormous span of time involved in this study I have included a brief index giving the chronological order of the dynasties against a background of approximate datings, major cultural developments, and historical fragments to be gleaned from surrounding lands. But it must be made quite clear at this juncture that where the earlier years are concerned there is really very little to go on. Actual documentary evidence is non-existent and we owe much of the more practical information to the dedicated work of archaeologists and, in more recent times, to those scientific teams who have spent many a tiring hour dating this object or that stone etc.

However, this is essentially a magical book, so we shall take one step further and lean a little upon magical sources of enquiry such as ESP, the psychic faculty, astral projection, hypnotic regression, and all the other fancy names given to the act of delving into the Akashic records.

Many years of experience in the study of altered states of consciousness – as these manifestations of the brain's ability to probe 'outer time' are now labelled – have shown me that the Egyptian ray is one which people either respond to readily and happily, or view with a suspicion bordering on unease. These attitudes stem from the subconscious and can be traced to the karmic past of the individual and, to a major degree, to their cosmic roots. It is my personal belief, and one shared by other occultists of my particular discipline, that those major civilizations that contributed in some way to the growth of magical understanding on this planet were 'seeded' from archetypal rays external to Earth. Recognizing which is which not only helps the counsellor to understand his subject, but also places into position a large missing chunk of the history of this planet and its place in the universal scheme of things.

I shall deal with Egypt's cosmic roots during the course of this study as the subject is highly relevant; but, first, let us examine the known traditions of Egyptian magic.

PART ONE
THE HISTORY AND THEORY

1. THE BOOK OF THE DEAD

The Book of the Dead was, to the Egyptians of old, something like the Bible is to modern day fundamentalist Christians, the inference being that it was taken too literally in later times, while the real meanings behind some of its teachings had become so obscured by the mists of antiquity that they bore no relationship or terms of reference to life in the later years.

The very title is, in fact, a misnomer, for its literal translation is *Chapters of the Coming Forth by Day*, and it would appear that the sole reason for referring to it as *The Book of the Dead* was on account of its deep concern with life after death and the preparation therefor.

Only fragments of this work, in the form that it has come down to us today, are actually concerned with magical ritual, whereas whole portions do refer to the state of the soul that has passed over and its trials and existences in other dimensions. In fact, more importance is placed upon what happens to us once we are dead and gone than on our welfare while still incarnate here. Shades of more contemporary beliefs, methinks. But one has also to take into account the fact that the ancient Egyptians, far from being 'pie in the sky' folks, were eminently practical, enjoyed a very ordered society, and did not spend their whole lives prostrating themselves before idols of cats, dogs, lions and the like. Fascinating looking but indecipherable sets of hieroglyphics that appeared to our forefathers to be mystical or magical wonders turned out to be simple invoices for so many barrels of

oil, wheat, fish or meat, plus a 'red notice' if the payment was
not forthcoming before the dog-days etc. All highly disillusion-
ing, but it told us one thing: those who possessed the true
magical knowledge did *not* leave it lying about amongst recipes
for smoked crocodile and requests for staff from the local
domestic agency. Did they, therefore, record it at all? One
wonders. Perhaps we should start looking into *The Book of the
Dead* and see what that tells us before we jump to any definite
conclusions.

My copies of this work are from a series entitled *Books on
Egypt and Chaldea*, by the late A.E. Wallis Budge, M.A.,
Litt.D., Keeper of the Egyptian and Assyrian Antiquities in the
British Museum, and the particular edition was published in
1901. The translations of the religious hymns and magical texts
are from a representative collection inscribed on the walls of
Egyptian tombs and sarcophagi, coffins and funeral stelae,
papyri and amulets. They were translated mainly from docu-
ments found at Thebes and taken together they are generally
termed the Theban Recension of *The Book of the Dead*, but
were originally entitled *The Chapters of Coming Forth by Day*.

The Theban dating, which was roughly 1600 B.C. to 900 B.C.,
was by no means the beginning, as we shall see, for *The Book of
the Dead – Das Todenbuch, Le Livre des Morts, Rituel
Funeraire,* to give it a few more names – is shrouded in deepest
antiquity. Its original Egyptian title was REU NU PERT EM
HRU, written thus in hieroglyphics:

One interesting fact. According to Budge, the book is definitely
not of Egyptian origin for, although it would appear that from
pre-dynastic times the aborigines of Egypt possessed tolerably
well defined ideas about the future life, they could not be
regarded as the authors even of the earliest Recension of *The
Book of the Dead,* because the work presupposes the existence
of ideas which the aboriginals did not possess and refers to an
elaborate system of sepulture which they never practised. But
who taught them these things no one knows for sure, historically
speaking, that is.

That these ideas were voluntarily borrowed from some other
nation or introduced by conquering immigrants has been con-

jectured by many scholars, but for centuries mystics and occultists have subscribed to the Atlantis theory and, in recent years, the suggestion that they were introduced by peoples from outer space has also found credence amongst many. One thing we do know for sure, if we are to rely upon the scholarship of historians like Budge, is that the original idea was brought to pre-dynastic Egypt externally and was definitely in existence thousands of years before the first dynasty.

The Heliopolitan Recension, or first section of it, was in use during the fourth and fifth dynasties and can be dated back to before 3500 B.C. Proof is offered by the mistakes in copying that the scribes of that period were dealing with texts which were, even in such remote times, so old as to be unintelligible in many passages. These copyists reproduced them without fully understanding their meaning, and thus inaccuracies inadvertently crept in. From descriptions given, these earliest records can be dated to a period when the banks of the Nile were overrun by prehistoric beasts hostile to man, and evidence is also contained therein indicating that climatic conditions described were far different from those encountered in recorded Egyptian history, or the history of the surrounding lands. In fact, Egypt is described as being damp and swampy.

These earlier fragments, which were so scrappily pieced together in times of antiquity, would appear to lend support to the theory of some kind of alteration in the Earth's axial rotation, which brought drastic changes to the climates of many lands. And so we find ourselves back with the biblical story of Noah and the flood and its corresponding legend in most other ancient cultures.

Evidence available archaeologically would appear to support the theory that the Egyptian aboriginals were stone and flint men, but that their conquerors used bronze and finely carved and worked metals. According to Budge, the early Egyptians owed to these immigrants the art of working metals, writing, building, pottery-making etc., as well as a complete religious and magical belief. In fact, the changes were all suspiciously too sudden and highly radical.

Later changes or additions in or to existing cultures show very clearly the varying known external influences on Egyptian life and culture, such as the Libyan, Arabian, Hyksos etc., and the points in time where the gods or magical customs of these sub-cultures intermingled with existing Egyptian strains are easy to distinguish, as we shall see shortly.

The oldest copy of *The Book of the Dead* now known to exist on papyrus is that written for Nu, the son of 'the overseer of the house or the overseer of the seal, Amen-hetep, and the lady of the house, Senseneb'. This extremely valuable document is dated to the early part of the eighteenth dynasty. Two versions of the sixty-fourth chapter are given, one much longer than the other, and to each version a note is appended assigning a date to the text which it follows. One version, it claims, was found in the 'foundations of the shrine of Hennu by the chief mason, during the reign of his Majesty the king of the South and North, Semti (or Hesepti), and that the longer version was found in the city of Khemennu (Hermopolis, the city of Thoth) upon a block of iron of the south, which had been inlaid with letters of real lapis lazuli under the feet of the god (Thoth) during the reign of his Majesty Men-kau-Ra (Mycerinus)' etc. Of the two statements one ascribes the finding of the chapter to the time of the first dynasty, and the other to the fourth dynasty. Both statements are correct, according to Budge, and the longer version was doubtless the later one. Osiris and Horus are well depicted in these versions, which speaks for their antiquity as deities and dates their religion back to the first dynasty and before.

During the second, third and fourth dynasties little is known about what happened to the sacred books. There are ideas that have been culled from fragments and later writings, but no real evidence of a practical nature to back them up. During the reign of Men-kau-Ra (Mycerinus), a king of the fourth dynasty, we are told that chapters XXXV, LXIV and CXLVIII were 'found' by one Heru-ta-ta-f, the son of Khufu, a gentleman who was latterly considered to have been of great learning. The probability is that like King Semti he revised or edited old chapters to which his name is attached in rubrics, as funeral inscriptions from that time evidence the existence of *The Book of the Dead* as being in general use. During the fifth and sixth dynasties a great development took place in funerary rites and ceremonies, and five selections of texts from this Recension have come down to us today.

These earlier texts are known as the Heliopolitan Recension because of the inclusion of views held by the priests of Annu or Heliopolis, but there would appear to be no just grounds for assuming that the five chapters that have come to us from that period constituted the entire work. In fact, the priests of Annu themselves effected many changes, and admitted so doing, probably because they had no idea what the original texts were all about and needed more practical terms of reference to relate the essence of their religion to the populace.

Between the sixth and eleventh dynasties the sacred books appeared to have become temporarily lost or abandoned and not until the eleventh dynasty did they reappear; but little is really known of the events that took place in the interval between the sixth and eleventh dynasties, for although in Upper Egypt tombs of considerable size and beauty made their appearance there were no outstanding changes in funeral procedures and no new Recension of *The Book of the Dead* was made.

The eleventh and twelfth dynasties threw up plenty of inscribed selections from the earlier Heliopolitan Recension, and these differed but little from the older character and contents of the fifth and sixth dynasties. In fact, there was a temporary return to the earlier ways, possibly the result of reaction against outside religious and political influences that had irked the populace in some way.

Between the twelfth and eighteenth dynasties we find another break in the history of this remarkable document and with the advent of the eighteenth dynasty the work entered a new phase in its existence, the transcriptions appearing now on papyri whereas they had formerly been seen only on coffins, sarco-phagi, pyramids etc.

It must be taken into account, of course, that economy played an important role as elaborate funeral arrangements were made only for royal personages or rich people anyway, so most of the earlier inscriptions that have come to us from pyramid writings, tombs or stone coffins were from those quarters of society. But as papyrus came into fashion for writing and was cheap by comparison with stone and more solid works, this was a time when any man who could read, write or afford a scribe could have his own copies made and his own invocations transcribed. It was the fashion for gentlemen to have inscriptions made for their wives or families, and this applied particularly to the priesthood.

The Egyptian priesthood was not a celibate one, neither was it given to excesses. They were a family orientated people, overall, and tended to look after the needs of their own both materially and spiritually.

The seat of these transformations was Thebes, city of the god Amen-Ra, and for this reason the Recension of *The Book of the Dead*, which was in common use from the eighteenth to the twenty-second dynasty, is known as the Theban Recension. Although the priests of Amen did little more than copy the texts of Annu to start with, as time went by they gradually incorporated the name of their own god, Amen, who slowly usurped the attributes of many of the older deities of Egypt. Amen, or Amon, was not a god native to Egypt and cannot be traced to the earlier dynasties. As father figure of the Theban triad he is usually partnered by the goddess Mut, and their son is the Moon god, Khonsu, often associated with healing. This is possibly a takeover from the earlier Memphis triad which consisted of the universal architect god, Ptah, patron of masons, his consort Sekhmet, the lion-headed one (sometimes Bast the cat goddess), and Nefertum/Imhotep, their son, who was also a healer god. I will deal with the gods and the principles they represent in a later chapter.

The texts of this dynasty were always written in black ink in vertical columns of hieroglyphics which are separated from each other by black lines, but titles of chapters etc. were written in red. Vignettes also came into common use during these times although there are records of their use as far back as the eleventh dynasty, so Thebes cannot lay entire claim to them.

Many famous papyri, such as the *Papyrus of Hunefer* (British Museum No. 9901), belong to this period, but the general feeling amongst scholars would appear to be that everything was sacrificed to colour and beauty at the expense of the old truths. Scribe and artist worked together to produce a vignette of colour and movement rather than a text of a teaching. Long copies of the Theban Recension were apparently made in sections and then joined together, and there are indications that few of the artists employed knew what the others were doing.

One of the finest illustrated papyri in existence, the *Papyrus of Ani*, omits a large section of text, which error was probably made by the scribe and not influenced by doctrinal changes or priestly interventions. Vignettes do have a special value in that they sometimes depict mythological scenes, gods' names etc. which do not occur elsewhere, and it is to these art forms that we owe much information concerning judgement scenes and the Egyptian concepts of karma. Another example of this is the *Papyrus of Anhai* from the twenty-second dynasty (British Museum No. 10,472), showing a vignette depicting the creation which does not relate to former texts from *The Book of the Dead*.

In the twenty-first and twenty-second dynasties there was a gradual decline in the artistic skill employed, and both the form and content of *The Book of the Dead* showed marked changes. Inaccuracies abounded and, according to Budge, instructions copied are grossly heretical.

From the twenty-second to the twenty-sixth dynasty we know nothing about religious or magical Egypt, probably because of the period of trouble and tumult through which the nation was passing. The priests of Amen-Ra, having engineered things so that their god usurped the position of all other gods including Ra himself, next usurped the kingdom on their own behalf but found themselves unable to maintain authority in the countries formerly conquered by the kings of earlier dynasties. Tributes imposed were refused, which resulted in the initial loss of temporal power and a final rebellion by the people themselves. Thus the rule of Amen finally came to a close.

With the rise of power of the kings of the twenty-sixth dynasty a general revival of the ancient religion took place. *The Book of the Dead* did not escape, and strong measures were taken by the scholars of the time to re-edit the work and clear away some of the Theban debris. The exact dating of this undertaking is not known, but it is generally believed that it was carried out by an assembly or college of priests specially appointed. The result of their labours was the Saite Recension of *The Book of the Dead,* or third phase in the history of this fascinating document, which naturally reflected strongly the religous views of the day.

The Saite Recension was in use in Ptolemaic times, but the scribes were then, or so it appears, completely ignorant of the meaning of the texts they copied and also the correct arrangement of the vignettes they added. Of special interest among the works popular in the Ptolemaic and Graeco-Roman period is the *Shai-en Sensen* or *Book of Breathings*. It presents ideas and beliefs derived from the older portions of *The Book of the Dead* and it is refreshing to note that, in spite of all the external conversions and inaccuracies produced by the passage of time, the fundamental concepts of the future life were roughly the same in the minds of the people.

The Book of the Dead was regarded by many as the inspirational work of Thoth, who was scribe to the gods; it was he, according to Egyptian belief, who spoke the words of creation which were then carried into effect by Ptah. All were in turn servants of Osiris.

In summary, the various Recensions of *The Book of the Dead* appear thus:

1. **The Heliopolitan Recension:** (a) That which was used in the fifth and sixth dynasties and is found inscribed in hieroglyphics upon the walls and chambers of the pyramids at Sakkara. (b) That which was written in cursive hieroglyphics upon the coffins in the eleventh and twelfth dynasties.

2. **The Theban Recension:** (a) That which was written upon papyri and painted on coffins in hieroglyphics from the eighteenth to the twenty-second dynasties. (b) That which was written in the hieratic character upon papyri in the twenty-first and twenty-second dynasties.

3. **The Saite Recension:** Which was written upon papyri, coffins etc., in the hieroglyphic, hieratic and demotic characters during the twenty-sixth and following dynasties. This was the Recension which was much used during the Ptolemaic period and may be regarded as the last form of *The Book of the Dead.*

In the *Book of Breathings,* in an address to the deceased it is said, 'Thoth, the most mighty god, the lord of Khemennu (Hermopolis), cometh to thee, and he writeth for thee the *Book of Breathings* with his own fingers.' Copies of *The Book of the Dead* were placed either in the coffin with the deceased or in some part of the tomb or mummy chamber, generally in a niche cut for them. Sometimes the papyrus was laid loosely in the coffin, but more frequently it was placed between the legs of the deceased, either just above the ankles or above the upper part of the thighs, prior to the swathing. Osiris usually appeared along with *The Book of the Dead* in the tomb, but also Ptah, in his role as god of resurrection, the implication being that whoever originally contributed to this renowned document in pre-Egyptian days was doubtless familiar with the law of entropy.

Having considered the bible of Egyptian belief, in the light of the knowledge available to us, let us now proceed to examine some of the more metaphysical concepts that went to make up the backcloth of Egyptian magic in those ancient days.

2. SPIRITUAL HIEROGLYPHICS

This is primarily a book about magical matters and I do not intend to embark upon a history of the development of the Egyptian hieroglyphic system of writing. There are many excellent text-books on the subject for those of scholarly inclination, and my employment of hieroglyphics will only be inasfar as they are related to spiritual or magical contexts. It is, however, important to examine the basic beliefs held in ancient Egypt regarding life after death, the journey of the soul and the purpose of life in the first place. At this point a great deal of sorting the wheat from the chaff is essential.

The subject of mummification is always a controversial one, as it can be argued that a people who placed so much significance upon the preservation of the physical vehicle couldn't have had much understanding of matters esoteric; and a valid point this is, too. Perhaps a deeper look into the character and psychology of this early race might throw a little light on the subject. As I have already explained, these were not basically a mystical people but essentially down to earth, which tendency inclined them to translate their gods into practical and easily understood imagery.

It has ever been the ego of man to fashion his deities in his own image and likeness and the ancient Egyptians were no exception, although they were, perhaps, a little broader-minded than modern day theologians in that they saw their gods in *all* creation and not just *Homo sapiens*. From studies I have made over the years, both esoteric and exoteric, it is my personal belief that the priests of the very earliest dynasties and, of course, those 'outsiders' from whom they originally gleaned their cosmic information did not teach the need for mummification but rather stressed the infinite and eternal nature of the soul.

Later generations, unable to conceive of immortality in some Elysian fields without a body with which to indulge in the more pleasant aspects of earthly existence, felt that some omission must have been made somewhere along the line and worked out an elaborate system for preserving the physical vehicle, in the sincere belief that one or other of the spiritual bodies would germinate or develop within it.

Mummification was not practised in pre-dynastic times. In fact, it was the done thing to cut up the bodies of the dead. This custom is echoed in the story of the body of Osiris which was supposedly severed into fourteen pieces and re-assembled by his wife/sister, Isis, who spoke magical words (as instructed by Thoth) over it, thus making it immortal.

The indigenous people of north Africa tended to dismember or burn their dead, and those bodies that were buried whole were laid on their left side with their head to the south with no attempt at mummification. There is ample evidence available regarding pre-dynastic burial customs which I will not pursue in detail in this work; suffice it to say that the necessity to preserve the physical body for life in some future world was not known or accepted in the very early days, and the later adoption of this strange custom appears to have arisen out of some misconception or misinterpretation of a more esoteric teaching, the true meaning of which had become obscured by time or lost in repeated translations.

What did they believe and how did they represent those beliefs?

The spiritual economy was something of an *entourage*, involving several 'vehicles' each of which partook of a specific function in the metaphysical scheme of things. First of all we have the *sahu* which was a form of etheric body. This could be utilized by the spirit after death for moving to the high planes, but the state of *sahu* could only be attained if certain prayers were said over the dead person. The god Osiris possessed a *sahu* himself and also had the power to bestow a similar vehicle on others, upon a suitably worded request, of course. The *sahu* could ascend to Heaven and dwell there with the gods. It was, in fact, an immortal vehicle and in it lived the soul.

The Sahu

The physical body was called a *khat*, i.e., that which was liable to decay and could only be preserved by mummification. It was written thus:

The Khat

Next we come to a more familiar term and its glyph, the *ka*, a word which by general consent is translated as 'double', the Coptic equivalent being ⲕⲱ and it can also be rendered by one of the meanings of εἴδωλον. The *ka* was an abstract personality which possessed the form and attributes of the man to whom it belonged and, though its normal place of residence was in the tomb with the body, it could wander about at will. Shades of Dracula and all that! Being independent of the body it could ensoul some inanimate object, such as a statue, or do a very good haunting job. The *ka*, the ancient Egyptians would have us believe, was partial to a tasty meal or glass of appropriate brew and care was taken to see that it was well catered for, in case it became hungry and went foraging around in dirty dustbins and taking nasty germs back to its nice, clean mummy.

The Ka

Now we come to the *ba*, or soul, which was in some inexplicable way connected with the *ka*, in whom, or with whom, it was supposed to dwell in the tomb. Highly companionable creatures, these spooks, for we are further informed that the *ba* liked to share a good meal with its *ka* friend when it wasn't away visiting Osiris in more exalted regions. The *ba* could visit the body whenever it pleased.

The Ba

Next we have the *ab*, or heart. This was closely associated with the soul and was held to be the source both of animal life and of good and evil in man. The preservation of the heart was considered to be of great importance and, in the Egyptian judgment, it was singled out for special examination. Sometimes it was even considered to be the centre of spiritual and thinking life and as the organ through which manifestations of virtue and vice revealed themselves. A good word for it might be 'conscience'. The *ab* suggests to me that somewhere way back along the line a knowledge of the chakras was possessed and the significance of the heart chakra or *anahata*, as related to human emotions (and the Isian archetype), was realized and understood.

The Ab

The *khaibit,* or shadow, follows next. It, in turn, was associated with the *ba* or soul and considered an integral portion of the human economy. Like the *ka* it appears to have been nourished by offerings and libations and it also had an existence apart from the body. Some crossed wires here, especially as they are all given as part and parcel of the one mummy.

The Khaibit

The *khu,* or spirit, is usually mentioned in connection with the *ba* or soul and seems to have been regarded as a shining thing which dwelt with the soul in the *sahu* or spiritual body.

The Khu

Next comes the *sekhem,* or power, said to be the personification of the vital force of the man. The *sekhem* dwelt in Heaven amongst the *khus* or spirits.

The Sekhem

Finally comes the *ren,* or name. The Egyptians took great measures to preserve the name for it was a widespread belief that, unless the name of a man was preserved, he would cease to exist. Again there is something in this consideration for, although we may not vanish into some parallel universe if somebody doesn't hail us occasionally, there is a strong meaning in the numerical significance of a name, as well as the actual sound of the word itself. Modern esoteric teachings subscribe to the belief that the vibration of a name is of the utmost importance and can make for harmony or disharmony in life.

The Ren

These hieroglyphics, plus those representing god-forms, are the most common to be found in tombs and burial chambers. Of course there are many others that are more connected with the day-to-day contingencies and life modes of the people who employed them. Although they were a devout people the Egyptians were not very inventive in the scientific sense; any skills they possessed in earlier times that did seep through to the later dynasties would appear to have been gleaned from some very advanced civilization of colonists who came out of the blue in pre-dynastic times and promptly (or so it would seem) vanished back into it. This statement in itself leaves a giant question mark, but I shall consider these debatable sources of Egyptian culture at a later stage in the proceedings.

There are many similarities between the Egyptian spiritual 'package' of bodies, shadows, names etc. and the series of similar vehicles taught in some modern (and extremely popular) schools of occultism. In most books on modern magic we are likely to encounter references to a company of astral bodies, etheric bodies, psyches, souls, egos, alter egos, spirits and ids. Even stone-faced materialistic psychologists rather like to play about with a series of identities which may or may not be part of our spiritual or psychological economy; all of which inclines me to agree with the views of American astrologer Zipporah Dobyns that the myriad personality forms now competing in modern psychology will quietly disappear as time progresses.

Perhaps we could boil things down to the level or density upon which the basic 'intélligence', or what have you, is operating at any given time. I have personally projected to give healing and been 'seen' standing beside a hospital bed by more than one person present, including non-believers. In my mind I was only 'thinking' myself there and visualizing the scene. But those who observed the phenomenon saw something more substantial than a fleeting thought. So possibly the Egyptians had something, except that I didn't stop *en route* for a cup of char from the tea trolley.

Recently there has been a craze to have one's name made up in Egyptian hieroglyphics and stamped out or engraved on cartouche-type jewellery. Nothing new under the Sun, is there? After all, we might forget our names one day, unless we change them in each life (which we no doubt do). So where would that take us? The occult significance of a name is more than the simple sound bestowed upon us by some unthinking parent at the time of any one of our births. It is the very vibration of the individual spark itself. I have heard it said that if a sonic, tuned exactly to the vibration of essence of a person, was touched off or sounded, that person would be instantaneously dissolved and, who knows, perhaps reassembled atomically in some other dimension or parallel universe in true 'Starship Enterprise' fashion.

The Egyptians subscribed to the efficacy of certain sacred words. There were words for opening doors to the hereafter, for invoking certain deities, for the retention of individuality (and the finding of same). These words gave rise to what became known in later occult systems as 'words of power'. Their association with a long lost knowledge of sonics is obvious, but then it always strikes me that so many 'magical' objects, beliefs and practices carry undertones, or overtones if you wish, of dim folk memories of some race that had achieved a high standard of science and technology the mechanics of which had long since been obliterated, leaving only a myth ...

3. ORIGINS

From our studies of *The Book of the Dead* it must be quite apparent that, at some point in their early history, the people of the Nile rubbed shoulders with a highly sophisticated and advanced culture that enjoyed a system of religious and magical beliefs different from anything they had formerly encountered.

Scholars disagree among themselves regarding the dates and time periods involved in pre-dynastic and early dynastic times. For example, according to Budge, the fourth and fifth dynasties existed approximately around 3500 B.C., while American expert James Bonwick, in his excellent book *Egyptian Belief and Modern Thought,* considers that the empire was founded about 5,000 years before the Christian era. Before King Menes, he states, the gods were said to have governed the country, which rather suggests that, whoever these people were who brought the civilizing light to the Egyptian lands in those far distant times, they ruled for a while and either took off again or, being few in number, were slowly absorbed into the indigenous population.

Before we proceed any further it might be a good idea to consider who these 'advanced people' might have been and whence they came. There is a lot of speculation and, as nobody knows for sure, much of what has been written and the theories put forward are purely academic. The more orthodox concept is of a small pocket of civilization evolving ahead of its surrounding cultures, possibly from Sumerian roots, and descending upon Egypt around 4000 B.C. As students of matters occult we must always keep an open mind and never discard a theory simply because it does not fit in with our pet concepts or flatter our egos as interpreters of the Akashic records. So we'll give that one the benefit of the doubt.

Theory number two involves the possible existence of an earlier civilization possessed of an advanced technology, which could equate with the Atlantis legend. Many books have been written about Atlantis and the pros and cons are legion. Plato started something with his story of this fabled land and squadrons of staunch Atlantean supporters have followed him down the centuries. The Victorian British Prime Minister, William Gladstone, was an avid believer in the lost continent, and in more recent times scientists on the other side of the iron curtain have added their support to the theory.

Atlantis has taken many forms in the minds of those who have espoused its Akashic cause. There have been vivid descriptions in novel form, usually 'recalled' under trance, hypnosis or simply ESP; theoretical arguments put forward by more practical-minded folk who have carefully noted geological/flora/fauna links and similarities between pyramidal structures on both sides of the Atlantic; and treatises by students of world geological history who have simply taken into account the logical sequence of the changing face of the planet over billions of years.

Atlantis has been seen by some as an island in the Mediterranean which was blown up around Minoan times; by others as the continent of Antarctica prior to the Ice Age and tilt of the Earth's axis which placed it in its present position in relation to the Sun; in the mid-Atlantic; in the north Atlantic; as part of Greenland; one could go on. Holders of these views have in turn been hotly pursued by the 'anti' writers, who make their name and money in providing a regular 'debunking' service to humanity. All very stimulating, no doubt, and in many cases highly necessary, or we would end up with an awful lot of bilge masquerading under suspect pseudo-scientific or ego-tripping mystical-religious banners. Your author has no intention at this stage (or any) of claiming infallibility (Heaven forbid she ever will) but, as this book unfolds, there will be plenty of evidence to help the student to decide for himself for, as an enlightened soul once stated, 'opinion is irrelevant to truth'.

The third, and probably most spectacular, consideration for

Egyptian spiritual and magical origins is a fairly recent one and involves the idea that people from outer space landed there and taught the primitives the basic arts of civilization. Writers in this field have used many of the existing beliefs to emphasize their point. We have had the 'sons of God and daughters of men' from the Bible; the flying machines from the Vedas; various communications from beings purporting to be from other planets (either incarnate or discarnate) and more recently the researches of Robert K.G. Temple. In his scholarly work, *The Sirius Mystery*, he examines in considerable detail the beliefs of the Dogons, an African tribe who live in Mali and for centuries have possessed a detailed knowledge of the Sirius star system, including its binary nature and additional satellites. Some of this information has only become available to science in recent years while a few of the finer points have yet to be substantiated. There would appear to be no way that these simple folk could have obtained this advanced knowledge unless it had been given to them, at some stage in the past history of their tribe, by someone or something with instruments capable of plotting and accurately recording the data. One suggestion is that the early Sumerians could possibly have invented a type of telescope consisting of a series of aligned lenses and that the Dogons were originally dwellers in the Mesopotamian area who later moved south, taking this Sumerian knowledge with them. Sirius was always an influencing factor in the life of the early Egyptians and they featured it both in their calendar and religion, the 'dog-days' being reckoned from its heliacal rising.

Mr Temple postulates that beings from the Sirius system visited Earth many thousands of years ago and were partly (if not entirely) responsible for the leap from primitive life to the high standard of culture and civilization achieved between the years 4500 B.C. and 3400 B.C. Nor is Temple alone in his 'space-origin' views, for several other writers with foresight enough to see threads linking science fiction with occult teachings have also hitched rides on this bandwagon. The space-arrival cult took off at rocket speed, much to the chagrin of those staunch occult traditionalists who saw our worldly roots in Lemuria, Atlantis or even dear old Stonehenge. Fortunately, science has dissolved many ideas from both sides in the acid of logic, but this has only had the effect of encouraging the human psyche to reach even further afield in search of cosmic roots.

Leaving scientific evidence (or the lack of it) out of the picture completely, there is a powerful school of occult thought that does support the theory that this solar system was seeded from Sirius, but whether this took as practical a form as Mr Temple suggests or whether the influence was purely a soul or spiritual one is again debatable. I have met several scientifically trained and normally level-headed people who subscribe to the idea that beings from Sirius genetically engineered the Atlantean race which in turn colonized Egypt. But, as I see it, the chronology is suspect if not uncertain. To quote an old axiom, however, there is 'no smoke without fire', so let us once more return to the little we do know about the early inhabitants of Egypt prior to the rise of the dynastic era.

Bonwick tells us that, whoever these immigrants were who appeared in Egypt at around 5000 B.C., they would have encountered a race of people who have been identified recently as being more of the Australian aborigine type than the Negro. They were a primitive but intelligent people with their own system of religion, superstition and magic. As we have already discussed, they did not mummify their dead, but their funeral rites were very similar to those discovered in surrounding lands for the same period. The newcomers (whoever they might have been) taught them to form communities, to work the land, make tools and instruments, develop a system of communication and observe certain basic laws. A new religion also appeared, although in some cases the prehistoric gods or spirits were allowed to exist side by side with the new deities. When dealing with magic in a later chapter I shall carefully separate the two, however, as this is highly important from an occult standpoint.

Magic can be classified into 'schools' or 'systems', each one of which carries the vibration of a certain archetypal ray. The powerful aspects of Egyptian magic stemmed not from the primitive and pre-dynastic religion of those lands but from the influence and culture of the colonizing strangers. As to where they came from I leave you, the reader, to make up your own mind.

4. THE GODS OF ANCIENT EGYPT

The Egyptian theological scene might appear at first glance to be a complex one, but this is not really the case. It is essential to bear in mind that we are dealing with two layers to start with, the primitive and nature deities of north Africa and the more archetypal god-forms into which they eventually became absorbed. During the passage of time numerous conquering peoples superimposed their own tribal gods over existing theologies, which resulted in what might appear to many to be a hotchpotch of polytheistic worship. But, even in the distant days of the past, there were enlightened souls who were perfectly capable of sorting the wheat from the chaff, as may be evidenced in traditions and fragments that have come down to us over the centuries. Of course, Egyptian magic and its accompanying *cultus* does leave much to be desired. But what system doesn't?

Sections of the Egyptian pantheon can be said to conform to the archetypal pattern of other early cultures, although there are aspects that do not slot easily into general correspondences as we shall examine in detail later. Of course it can be argued that an archetype, manifesting through any given civilization or culture, will automatically assume an overlay relative to the individuality or idiosyncrasies of the indigenous people in question. Thus, a maternal archetype appearing in a patriarchally-orientated culture would tend to manifest more domestically than it would amongst a matriarchal people, where it might assume religious identity as a wisdom goddess or perhaps a protective warrior, or in a balanced society where it could even emerge in masculine form.

Bearing this in mind, let us examine the records available from one of the earliest known cities in Egypt, Heliopolis, which name would appear to have solar connotations in both the Egyptian and Greek languages, hinting, perhaps, at some common philological origin. Here we encounter a very important group of gods known as the Divine Ennead of Heliopolis. But it is necessary to delve even further back into antiquity to discover the family of deities from which the Heliopolitan ennead originally sprang. The first of these ancestral divinities to receive mention was an abstract personality known as Atum or Tem, who appears as a sort of formless spirit that existed prior to the creation of the Earth.

The ancient Egyptians were past masters at matching or marrying up their gods. It simply wasn't decent, they felt, for a highly respected deity to be without a mate, consort or whatever and, if progeny could be added, so much the better. So dear old Atum was duly married off to an equally abstract goddess named Nebhet-Hotep who obligingly bore him the twin gods, Shu and Tefnut. Shu is usually depicted in human form while Tefnut, his sister, is always shown as a lioness. According to some authorities, however, both were originally leonine deities, being the twin lion gods who guarded the gates to the kingdom of Osiris.

Esotericists would doubtless inform us that the legend's message concerned the blending of two primary principles to produce two further archetypal rays ultimately destined to become involved in the growth and development of this solar system, but there are also some rather more way-out theories about civilizations of advanced intelligence and high technological advancement, external to this Earth, who did not, perhaps, look exactly like us.

Another explanation is that Atum and his beloved were simply theological concepts and their leonine progeny represented the strength to be gained by worshippers who sought their tutelary services.

Moving on a bit further, or should I say descending from the clouds, we come to the best known of all Egyptian gods, Ra or Re, the creator and sovereign lord of the sky. His sacred object was the obelisk, Ben-Ben, and his temple was called 'the place of the obelisk'. Legend has it that Ra manifested on Earth as an obelisk and it was through this stone that he was able to infuse intelligence into creation; this 'creation' referred *not to little old Earth but to a much larger area of stars*, indicating that he was not, in fact, the deity of our solar disk at all.

Many believed Atum and Ra to be one and the same, Ra simply being a more manifest version of Atum. It was said that in his early days he lived in the primordial lotus in the primordial ocean that was called Nun. However, one day he grew weary of the water and rose in all his splendour as Ra. After being responsible for the birth of Shu and Tefnut he seems to have withdrawn into a more 'heavenly father' role.

It is interesting to consider that somewhere amid this cosmogony a thread of science follows through. The atomic sequence from hydrogen to helium, for example, or the evolution of life from the sea. For those with the time and curiosity to examine these principles in a more scientific light there is a wealth of information to be gained. But this book is a magical one so I must not digress.

Shu and Tefnut united to bear the gods Geb and Nut (Earth and Sky) and, from the alliance of Geb and Nut, Isis and her family eventually issued forth, which brings us back to the ennead of Heliopolis. This group of gods is presented in different forms and with different names. We have, for example, one record which lists them as Ra, Shu, Tefnut, Geb, Nut, Osiris, Isis, Set and Nephthys. Another reference gives the names as Thoth, Horus, Bast, Anubis, Osiris, Isis, Nephthys, Ptah and Hathor/Sekhmet. Hathor is somewhat enigmatic at the best of times. Some scholars define her in the dual role of the benign cow on the one hand and the avenging lioness on the other; other authorities staunchly claim that she has no connection at all with the lion figure which was an earlier version of Bast. In my own experience I have found the Bast and Hathor influences to be entirely different and I shall be covering these aspects of the study in Part II of this work.

A very definite story is woven around the histories of the early Egyptian gods; to see the whole picture we will need to pick up the threads of what happened to Ra prior to the arrival on the scene of Isis and her family. We are told that he reigned peace-fully over all creation while he was still young and strong but, as

he aged, a group of dissenters moved to take advantage of him.
We are not told who these beings were or whence they hailed;
the inference is that they were not necessarily connected with
this Earth as we know it but were more like players in some
cosmological drama. Ra was so enraged at this uprising that he
hurled his divine eye at the revolutionaries in the form of the
goddess Sekhmet (the lioness goddess whom some believe to be
an aspect of Hathor) who emerges at this point as Ra's
daughter. Sekhmet went among the evil ones dispensing havoc
and bloodshed until Ra finally called her off, fearing that she
might overdo things a bit and polish off his handiwork entirely.
There are several conflicting legends as to how she was finally
persuaded to withdraw but, as these are not totally relevant to
her archetypal role, I shall not take up space by mentioning
them.

The ingratitude of the beings he had created gave Ra a
distaste for the world so he withdrew to Heaven and, on the
orders of Nun, the goddess Nut changed into a cow and carried
him away on her back. She raised him high in the vault of
Heaven and at that time the *present world,* our Earth, was
created.

Can we deduce from this story that it related to another solar
system – Mr Temple's Sirius, perhaps – with the ageing process
and eventual collapse of the secondary or binary sun from the
state of being a bright orb, like its stellar companion Sirius 'A',
to the white dwarf that it is at present? Did the legend also tell
the people that some force or energy was released at the time of
this occurrence, possibly from the immense nuclear reaction that
coincided with the ensoulment, if not the actual birth, of our own
solar system? It is always advisable to consider any superstition
as being a distant corruption of what was once a scientific fact;
after all, history leaves us with so many unanswered questions
about the evolution and development of *Homo sapiens* and
science is constantly unearthing evidence which takes the origin
of life even further back into the mists of time. Just as we now
laugh at the Victorian concept of 'Adam and Eve and all that'
occurring around 4000 B.C., future generations may smile at our
ignorance as they print their history books, with figures
stretching back into stellar periods so immense that our present
limited thinking modes would be completely nonplussed by
them.

Poor old Ra seems to be constantly cropping up in Egyptian theology in one form or another. Later generations of Egyptians saw Osiris as the incarnation of the supreme solar deity; then Horus, as son of Osiris, assumed the god-role in much the same way as certain gods in eastern faiths manifest in teacher or redeemer aspects from time to time. In addition to the previously mentioned and somewhat ambiguous dissenters who made a nuisance of themselves with the Sun god, Ra's only real enemy was the serpent Apep, a representation, no doubt, of the eternal force of evil or darkness; but in his early days Ra was defended from this obscenity by his daughter Bast, the cat goddess. It is interesting to note that both Bast and Sekhmet are referred to in the old texts as daughters of Ra, although at a later date Bast appears as twin sister to Horus and therefore daughter of Isis and Osiris. It is obvious that we are dealing with the same principle under different names.

Heliopolis was the sacred city of the Sun god, hence its name. In addition to the nine gods or ennead, already named, the religion of Heliopolis incorporated several other divinites. Perhaps these were simply local nature godlings, accommodated in much the same way that Christianity utilized existing pagan deities and their festivals to spread their own doctrines during the first few centuries A.D. The story of the family of Ra continues through Shu and Tefnut, eventually leading up to the arrival of Isis and her kin.

Shu and his sister Tefnut were twins. Shu was the Atlas of Egypt, his role being to support the sky; he was also depicted as a warrior when he was known by the name of Anhur. Tefnut, the lioness, was goddess of the Sun and dew; legend had it that she received the new born Sun each morning.

Shu and Tefnut's children, Geb and Nut, apparently upset their grandfather, Ra, in some unexplained way. In his anger the old god decreed that they should not bear a child in any month of the year. The couple were greatly distressed by this and sought the help of Thoth, the magician. Having pity on their plight, Thoth played a game of draughts with the Moon and, in the course of several games, he won a seventy-second part of the Moon's light with which he composed five new days. As these days did not belong to the official Egyptian calendar of 360 days Nut was able to give birth successively to five children: Osiris, Isis, Horus, Nephthys and Set.

What a fascinating story and what a challenge it presents to the enquiring mind. To me it suggests that Geb (the sky) and Nut (the Earth) became in some way out of alignment with the Sun, which prevented the planet from settling into a productive and stable orbit. Thoth, deva of time and magic and keeper of the Akashic records, helped them to right matters, but in order to do this he had to juggle with the Moon. This would seem to have had the effect of slightly altering the angle of the Earth in relation to the Sun and so increasing the year from 360 to 365 days. Ancient calendars show a time when the Sun rose and set in a different place from that which we now observe; so the myth would appear to relate to a period in the Earth's past history when there was a change in its axial rotation, possibly causing floods and dramatic alterations in climate throughout the planet, all this being well covered in the myths and legends of most lands. The Egyptians were merely observing and converting to story form a series of cosmological changes involving the Moon; possibly, also, the arrival of a new era in the history and evolution of this planet.

Many students of the occult are of the opinion that the inclusion of the intercalary days coincided with the sinking of Atlantis and that the five gods and goddesses mentioned as being born during those five days were simply rulers from the old country who went to Egypt, taught the indigenous population all that we have previously discussed and eventually passed away. No doubt the other school of thought would insist that these deities were space people who arrived in those troubled times to re-establish civilization and do a spot of genetic engineering before piling back into their spacecraft and heading for the Sirius system, or wherever. As the saying goes: 'You pays your money and you takes your pick.'

This brings me to the most important set of deities in the whole Egyptian pantheon, the principles that form the foundation of Egyptian magic:

Osiris. The Greeks called him Pluto or Dionysus. He was a nature god and a king, the universal lord. According to tradition he abolished cannibalism, taught the solar religion, taught men to produce grain etc., built temples with fine images and laid down strict religious laws. He also built towns, gave mankind civilization and invented two kinds of flute to accompany ceremonial songs. He was always accompanied on his travels by his grand vizier, Thoth, and his nephew (or some say his son), Anubis. Isis was his wife and Horus his son. Osiris is always depicted with a greenish face and dressed in white. He carries a crook and flail, the insignia of order and discipline, and is sometimes shown seated on a throne, surrounded by water from which grows the primordial lotus. His symbol is the djed, or tet, a stylized tree.

Isis, or Aset (Isis being the Greek version of Aset), which simply means 'a throne', the symbol worn on the head of this goddess; like her husband, Isis was also a highly civilized being and a great ruler in her own right. She taught men to grow corn (a grain sacred to her), to spin cloth and make garments for themselves. She instituted marriage and instructed her people in the art of healing disease.

In order to understand Egyptian magic fully it is necessary to know the legend of Isis and Osiris, as this has been the inspiration behind the Egyptian magical system since the dawn of history. Those of scholarly inclination will no doubt have recourse to Plutarch for the details, but here is the tale in essence:

Osiris and his sister/wife, Isis, ruled over the lands later called Egypt. They were both divinities from Heaven (?) who had descended to Earth to aid the development of mankind. Osiris had a brother, Set (Typhon), and the two brothers dwelt amicably with their wives, Isis and Nephthys, in Abydos. Osiris was much loved by the people, having taught them the arts of civilization; he promoted piety, good health and well-being amongst them.

While travelling to visit south-east Asia (some say India) with his wife, Osiris was suddenly summoned by his brother to return. During his absence Set had conspired with seventy-two others (that number seventy-two again) who arranged a banquet to celebrate the King's homecoming. As part of the entertainment a strange box was introduced and, one after the other, the guests tried to fit into it. Only Osiris was able to slide comfortably inside, upon which move the conspirators shut and sealed the lid. We are told that Osiris entered the box or tomb on 7 Athyr (13 November), the very day and month when Noah was supposed to have boarded the biblical ark. The box was then thrown into the Nile, or the sea, and carried onwards by the inundation. Eventually it was caught up in a tamarisk tree.

Isis, who had been visiting Chemnis, received news of what

had occurred. She hastily summoned her nephew Anubis and set out to seek for her husband's body. At Byblus she found the tree, but it was guarded by a magical power and she could not approach the coffin. As she watched, the King of Byblus came looking for a tree to serve as a column for his palace. He selected the very one that held Osiris. In vain did Isis, in her form as a dove, utter plaintive cries to dissuade the men from cutting it down, so she resumed her womanly appearance and went to the palace where she became nurse to the Queen's child.

By ingratiating herself with her employers Isis was able to match the evil magic of Set and secure the coffin. But her troubles were far from over. Set heard about her deeds and artfully stole the box while she slept. He opened the coffin and cut the body of Osiris into fourteen pieces, dispersing them in various places. Isis then had the task of seeking each piece. With her sister Nephthys and her nephew Anubis she travelled far and wide until she had located every piece except the phallus. This had been eaten by an oxyrhynchus, although some say by a spider. She then made a phallic likeness from wood and brought the whole body to Abydos for burial. Together with Nephthys, her sister, Anubis, her nephew, and Thoth, her uncle, Isis wept bitterly over her dead husband and chanted magically. So powerful were the tears and prayers, and the occult powers of Thoth, that one member of Osiris began to evidence vitality and secured conception for the faithful wife. Osiris then ascended to Heaven from which sublime place he continued to watch over Isis while she carried and bore his only son, Horus.

Although this part of the legend tells us that Horus was born in this miraculous way, in other texts he is simply a reincarnation of his father; there is even a tale that he was conceived by Isis and Osiris while they, too, were in the womb of their mother and unborn. This last suggestion would, no doubt, be happily welcomed by those who see the Osirian family as hailing from outer space and arriving, plus baby, in a UFO.

However, to continue the myth: Set, realizing that the child Isis carried was to be the avenger of his father, resolved to destroy them both. But Isis, through the aid of magic, skilfully avoided her pursuers. Some say she went to live on the Sun, others that she dwelt beneath the sea where the sea nymphs protected her. The more down-to-earth story is that she fled to a small island on a lake near Buto, where her son was born. In loneliness she reared her child, who was sickly to start with but gradually grew to mature strength. Upon reaching manhood Horus went forth to right matters with Set. A great contest took place in the plain beyond Siout and Horus carried off the laurels.

Horus restored the throne to Isis but she refused the position, placing her son in the seat of rulership before returning to Heaven to join the spirit of her husband. Horus then took to wife Hathor, or some say Bast, his twin sister, and everybody lived happily ever after. In spite of Horus's victory the Egyptians continued to fear Set and he came to be identified as their 'devil' or personification of the forces of evil; in his guise as the serpent Typhon — enemy of Ra — he is often portrayed fleeing before a pursuing Horus who is armed with lance at the ready in true St George fashion, or being chopped up with a large knife by Horus's sister, Bast, in her cat form.

As this whole story would appear to encompass an enormous span of time, many are tempted to believe that it related to the complete history of this Earth and not simply to an event from the past of Egypt. The aeon of Horus is the Aquarian Age, say the mystical sages, a time when the son of Isis will return to avenge his father, do away with Set and bring peace, light and love to all mankind. We love it! What we have been enduring for the past few centuries equates with the wanderings of Isis in the wilderness while Horus grew in strength and wisdom. It all sounds tremendously promising when viewed in that light.

The fourteen pieces of Osiris for which Isis sought can be equated with the power centres or chakras of the Earth; or perhaps with those much discussed 'time capsules' which are supposedly programmed to come to light at appropriate times in the Earth's history. There are all sorts of ways in which the myth can be interpreted, so before we get into too much hot water I'll return to my descriptions of the gods and their attributes.

Isis was a magician, possibly the archetype for the high priestess of the tarot. She learned her magic from Thoth, although according to some legends she obtained her powers from Ra himself by tricking him into revealing his name to her, thus acquiring his full magical knowledge. We have already discussed the magic of names, so it is easy to see how this idea arose. The goddesses Isis and Hathor are often confused. The earliest representations of Isis depict her crowned with the throne ◢▰, which is correct. The horned disk was Hathor's symbol and only merged with the Isian headgear in later dynasties. The symbols of Isis are the throne, the tat, knot or buckle, and the sistrum. She shares the latter with Hathor and Bast. Her colour is clear sky-blue.

Set, brother of Osiris and Isis, was the Egyptian 'baddie'. He was supposed to have had red hair, which made red an evil colour in Egyptian magic and one which was never used in the service of light. He stands for the forces of chaos and destruction, or energy misplaced. He was the manifestation of Apep or Typhon, opposers of the power of light. In magical practice Set is generally considered to represent the dualistic side of each of the other rays in common usage. In other words, he is the anti-ray that will cancel out, or destroy, if allowed any form of prominence.

Nephthys, whom the Greeks sometimes thought of as Aphrodite or Venus, was the sister and wife of Set, but did not support him in his persecution of Osiris. In fact, she left him and espoused the cause of Isis. According to some sources she seduced Osiris in order to have a son and Anubis was the result of this strange union (not that Isis minded at all, it seemed).

What we are really being told is that the principles represented by these rays, when united, produce a third principle. Osiris represented light and truth, and Nephthys, the revealer, psychic receptivity. The Egyptian magi were simply stating that, when light and truth unite with revelation, a force is brought into being that will guide us through the dark regions of the underworld in safety. In other words, in order to negotiate the uncharted realms of altered states of consciousness we must develop the Anubis within us etc. Nephthys is the guardian of things hidden or concealed, which includes any form of invisibility or obscurity. Those wishing for anonymity should choose her as their tutelary goddess. Her colours are pale green or silver and her symbols the lotus and the cup or chalice. Her Egyptian name is Nebhet and she is depicted with a basket or container on her head. She is often considered as a 'dark' goddess and some authorities see her as the hidden side of Isis and not as an individual archetype in her own right. This is totally incorrect. However, care should be taken not to confuse the idea of 'dark' meaning 'obscure' with any unpleasant connotation that word may have for more orthodox religious-minded folk.

Horus. There were two Horuses according to some writers; one equated with Shu and the other was Horus, son of Isis. Doubtless we are dealing with the same archetype all the way through, the differences having sprung from local colour and interpretation. Horus equates with the Greek Apollo and his colour is clear yellow or gold. He appears in several archetypal guises, sometimes as the warrior avenging the death of his father, as lord of prophecy, as god of music and art and, being extremely handsome himself, as patron of all things beautiful to behold. The prophecy that he will return to re-establish the solar cycle of his father with the help of his wife Hathor/Sekhmet or Bast is believed by many to presage the Aquarian Age. His symbols are the hawk and the all-seeing eye. The cat family is also closely associated with him as Bast was called his twin sister.

Hathor (Athyr), who is also associated with Aphrodite, was the daughter of Ra and carrier of his divine eye. Hathor was a dual-aspected goddess: as the benign celestial cow she was said to nourish the gods, protect women, patronize the art of astrology and confer the creature comforts of life. She is also called 'the lady of the sycamore' and was said to preside over all aspects of women's beauty such as make-up, adornment, jewellery etc. But according to some authorities Hathor has another side as Sekhmet, the lioness-headed goddess. Perhaps the ancients were simply trying to tell us that energy can either heal and nourish, when used *constructively*, or break and destroy if used *destructively*. Like most warrior goddesses (as opposed to warrior gods) she tended only to fight in defence, or to right a wrong on behalf of someone she loved, which is also typical of the Greek goddess Athene (wisdom), the most powerful of all warriors; this is another way of saying that wisdom ultimately conquers force. Even in her Sekhmet form this goddess could be benign and just; it is as the lioness-headed lady that she some-times appears in the Memphis triad, together with Ptah and Imhotep (or Nefertum), god of healing. A monument tells us that her worship is of such antiquity that when Cheops restored her temple at Denderah in 3500 B.C. it was in crumbled ruins. Her colours are coral, peach shades and copper. The mirror or shield is sacred to her and she shares with Isis a liking for the sistrum.

Anubis, the 'go-between' this world and the next, is usually represented as a dark-coloured Egyptian hunting hound, or a jackal. He is the traditional guardian against the forces of the lower astral and partakes of some of the nature of Cerberus. Patron of anaesthetics, psychiatrists and anyone looking for lost things, Anubis, as the guide dog, leads the seeker to his mother, Nephthys the revealer, or to Osiris in the halls of judgment. It was customary to invoke him before any form of surgery or hospital treatment that required a period of being 'under', as it was believed that he guarded the spirit, or *ba*, while it was away from its physical shell and helped it to return safely after the medical treatment had been administered. Terracotta is his colour and his symbol the sarcophagus or coffin (sometimes depicted as a box or column).

Thoth, or Tehuti, is one of the most interesting of all the early Egyptian gods and is often referred to as the uncle of the family. He is depicted in some vignettes as the dog-headed baboon but mostly as an ibis-headed man. Thoth is the god of medicine (the Greek Hermes), learning, magic, truth, books and libraries, keeper of the Akashic records, time lord etc. In some records he is considered to be the child of Nun, which would make him the brother of Ra with obvious connections with another solar system. Another legend tells us that at his word the four gods and goddesses came forth and that it was he who spoke the sacred words which released to Ptah the energy necessary to effect the creation of the universe. (Shades of the St John gospel: 'In the beginning was the Word ...') In *The Book of the Pyramids*, one of the oldest on record, Thoth is spoken of as being the eldest son of Ra; in other texts he is the brother of Isis and Osiris. His voice is said to have magical properties. It was he, as the divine judge, who ruled in favour of Horus against Set, following their famous contest. Patron of history, keeper of the divine archives, lord of karma, herald of the gods, his female aspect is Maat, goddess of truth, often personified individually. Sometimes he is said to have been married to Maat but, according to other legends, his wife was Seshat, a star goddess who was patroness of architects and taught men to build by the stars. It is the opinion of most experts, however, that all these were merely aspects of the god himself and not individual deities. His symbols are the white feather and the caduceus, his colour is amethyst and the ibis is sacred to him.

Bast or Bastet/Pasht, whom the Greeks equated with Artemis, is also considered to be an aspect of Tefnut or

Sekhmet. As the wife of Ptah, there is a definite connection between Bast and the lion-headed deities. The priests of Egypt seriously believed her to be the sister of Horus and daughter of Isis and Osiris. Bast, like Horus, was a goddess of music and dance; the sistrum was her sacred instrument and the cat her animal. In her earliest form she was known as 'Pasht' and there is mention of her in records dating back to 3000 B.C. It was in later dynasties, however, that her worship flourished and the ceremonies of Bubastis are well recorded by Herodotus for those interested enough to read about them.

The Memphis Triad

Memphis was prominent in earlier times and its occult disciplines have carried through to present day masonry. The triad consisted of Ptah, Sekhmet (or Bast) and Nefertum/Imhotep.

Ptah. This gentle artisan god was patron of builders and craftsmen and his title 'architect of the universe' speaks clearly of his masonic associations, even in those early times. He performed miracles and was much loved and understood by the ordinary people. Some consider him to be an aspect of Osiris, but from my own magical experience I would assign him an archetypal individuality of his own. His symbols are the mason's tools and cord.

Sekhmet, his wife, was shown with the head of a lioness crowned with the Sun disk. As we have already discussed, Sekhmet also appeared as Hathor, the nourisher, but it was in her lioness form that she was espoused to Ptah. Some scholars are of the opinion that Sekhmet and Bast are the same archetype and not Sekhmet and Hathor. If this were so, the syzygy of Horus/Hathor as a husband and wife team and Horus/Bast as brother and sister would no longer appear as enigmatic. However, at this stage I shall simply state the evidence available and we will sort out the application of the principle when we come to the subject of practical magic.

Nefertum, son of Ptah and Sekhmet, wears a lotus on his head. Legend had it that he guarded the Sun at night. Later, his position as third member of the trinity was usurped by Imhotep, the physician god. The Greeks were of the opinion that Imhotep equated with their own god of medicine, Aesculapius, or even Hermes, and archaeological evidence is tending to lend support to the idea that a person of this name and attributes actually existed, was buried in great splendour and later deified in much the same way that certain branches of Christianity canonize their saints because of miracles purportedly originating from their relics.

The Theban Triad

A very important group of gods, this, and one which greatly influenced the history of Egypt. It consisted of Amon (Amen or Amun), Mut his consort and their son Khonsu.

Amon was identified by the Greeks with their sky god Zeus. He was adopted by the Thebans from more humble sources. Some say he arrived in Egypt with the Hyksos and was, therefore, one and the same as Jehovah or Yaweh; according to other sources Thebes was once a village and Amon its local primitive deity. In the famous eighteenth dynasty Amon reigned supreme, his name becoming affixed to that of the reigning pharaoh as an indication of the ruler's divinely appointed position. The exception was Amenhotep IV, later named Akhnaton, who didn't approve of Amen and tried hard to eliminate his worship from the religious system of the day. His special god-form was Aten, an abstract concept represented by a solar disk, and his famous 'hymn to Aten' is classified amongst the great poetic works of early history. Akhnaton died under rather suspect circumstances and when his son-in-law, the much publicized King Tutankhamen, ascended the throne the powerful priests of Amon assumed control once again, allowing their deity to usurp the mantle of Ra himself. Amon is depicted with a ram's head (Arien Age?) and his name means 'hidden'.

Mut, the consort of Amon, was identified by the Greeks with their goddess Hera. But she is really a vague and ill-defined deity whose name simply means 'mother'.

Khonsu, the navigator, was apparently adopted by Amon and Mut as they had no son of their own. Khonsu was a gentle god, renowned for his therapeutic powers and literary inclinations. His statues were said to create healing miracles. Associated with the Moon, he was compassionate and kind by nature and not at all unlike the third member of the Memphis triad, Imhotep, whose properties he had no doubt assumed.

I will now list some of the other gods and goddesses, but purely for general information, as few if any of them have places of importance in the magical scheme of things.

Harmarkhis, the god name for the sphinx, is also said to be another aspect of Horus. There has been much speculation concerning the significance and function of this edifice, both from a metaphysical and a scientific standpoint. It would certainly appear to have strong occult connotations that are possibly associated with Siriun magic and the long standing relationship between hominids and the lion family that predates this solar system by countless eons of time.

Wepwawet, shown as a jackal but quite distinct from Anubis, was of a warrior-type nature and was possibly a local primitive concept whose true origins have become obscured by the mists of time.

Nekhebet, equating with the Greek Eileithyia, goddess of childbirth, would appear to fit snugly into the category of supernaturals who were simply primitive personifications of ideas or principles.

Buto was the snake goddess who befriended Isis. Again, this name originated from the name of the place where Isis was said to have hidden to escape the wrath of Set, the inference being that we are dealing purely with a place name and not an actual theological concept at all.

Mont was a real 'oldy' adopted from primitive times and later dropped completely. He was an old Mu-an Sun god from all accounts.

Neith was protectress of Sais; her sign was crossed arrows on an animal skin, which tempted the Greeks to tie her in with Athene. A very ancient deity, Neith more than likely equated with Nut, or even Isis. The weaver's shuttle was also symbolically sacred to her.

Knumm, sometimes seen as a ram or goat, was the divine potter who fashioned the world; a much loved god, gentle and constructive, whose wives were Sati and Anuket. Logically, we can assume him to be an aspect of Ptah that was given a local name.

Harsaphes, also a ram-headed deity, which dates him to the Arien period, is again a good example of a local primitive essence creeping into a more sophisticated theology.

Min was associated with both Pan and Horus. He was a god of vegetation and the thunderbolt was his emblem although he

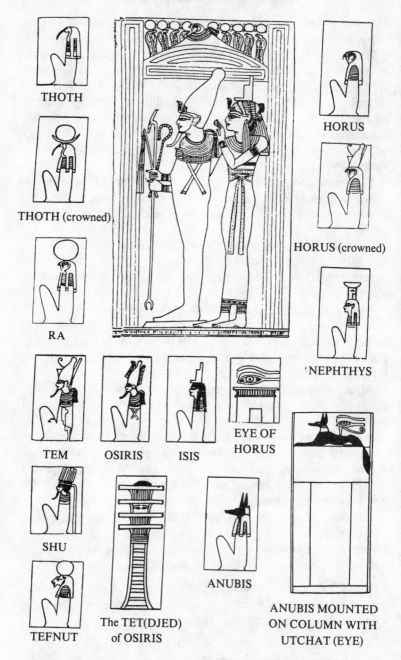

THOTH

THOTH (crowned)

RA

HORUS

HORUS (crowned)

'NEPHTHYS

TEM   OSIRIS   ISIS

EYE OF
HORUS

SHU

TEFNUT

The TET(DJED)
of OSIRIS

ANUBIS

ANUBIS MOUNTED
ON COLUMN WITH
UTCHAT (EYE)

Some representations of the gods from *The Book of the Dead* (Budge)

was essentially a fertility god bearing no relationship at all to Zeus.

Hapi was the divine name for the Nile; **Apet** the hippo goddess who looked after maternity; **Heket** a frog goddess, patroness of midwives.

The **Hathors**, not related at all to the goddess of that name, were fairy godmothers of a sort, who appeared at the birth of famous people or those born to a great destiny. They equate with those Christian angels who 'announce'.

Shai was not really a god at all, it was simply the name for destiny.

Renenet was an old Mu-an divinity who was said to nourish babies during their nursing period.

Khepera, the scarab, was the deity of transformation, probably a purely theological concept, using a life form – i.e., the scarab beetle – as an example that primitive people could be made to see and understand. The scarab often assumed magical importance as the uninitiated believed there to be some mystery about its procreative habits.

Renpet was the goddess of spring and growth; **Bes**, clown or jester to the gods, a dwarf at whose deformities less enlightened folk might see fit to laugh, which definitely dates him to primitive times as the Isis/Osiris group were essentially kind and benign.

Selket, the scorpion goddess, was guardian of married couples.

The four sons of Horus were really the four elements. They were born in a lotus and always appeared in judicial scenes with Osiris, as though judging how the soul had treated the four elements during that life. Their names are:

   Imsety (with a human head) – water
   Hâpi (with an ape head) – earth
   Duamutef (with a jackal head) – fire
   Qebhsnuf (with a hawk head) – air

Ament, although included amongst Egyptian deities, was, in fact, Libyan.

Mertseger was not a god at all, the name simply meant 'silence'.

Maat was, as already stated, a theological concept of truth as represented by the feather. Possibly a female aspect of Thoth or Tehuti.

Nehet was the name for eternity.

There were many sacred animals, the most famous of which was probably the bull of Apis. Said to be a personification of Osiris, Apis was much honoured in later times, as was also the goat of Mendes and the bennu bird. But all these creatures were doubtless carry-overs from the animal emblems of the different 'nomes' or divisions of the country prior to its unification.

There are many books available which deal simply with the gods, their many legends and precise history. I do not have the space to indulge in this form of scholarship, but the public libraries are well stocked with relevant literature for those who really want the finer details.

My coverage of the gods has been brief and abridged; it is simply a guide to a better understanding of what the real magical forces of ancient Egypt were and how they can be separated from local, natural and sympathetic magic. Of course, all magical systems have their points of efficacy, but in Egypt we are dealing with something rather more, as we shall see.

5. THE REAL THEOLOGY

From the foregoing chapters it might strike the casual observer as facetious that a people so primitive as to be misled into divers polytheistic beliefs could possibly possess any real knowledge of human psychology, let alone have a grasp of the divine. But this couldn't be further from the truth. For one thing, the polytheism that appears so obvious at first glance does not hold good under closer scrutiny. Many individualized Egyptian deities were simply aspects of the one divine archetype, and minor gods were of no more importance than the Catholic saints who are prayed to for this or that favour, according to their earthly deeds and inclinations. The recently demoted St Christopher has much in common with the Egyptian Anubis, for example, and many a lonely traveller carried an emblem of the guide-dog god to see him safely to his destination. St Thomas Aquinas, like his Egyptian counterpart Thoth, is also invoked by earnest students about to sit theological examinations and, after all, both were magicians in the truest sense of the word.

There are countless other examples which go to prove that people haven't changed much over the centuries. We all have a basic psychological need, whether it be for a form of spiritual strap to hang onto in times of stress, a scapegoat to rid us of our guilty feelings, or simply something beyond the normal senses which we deem to be a cut above earthly weaknesses and therefore worthy of our respect and worship.

The Egyptians believed in the priest, or professional religious

man, and his power to produce effects. They did not exclude
women from the priesthood. In his daily life the priest was as
sober and moral as any Christian and he was not so prejudiced.
The Egyptians had a healthy respect for the animal and plant
kingdoms, which is more than can be said for many a
religiously-bigoted group today. They had inherited their deeper
beliefs from a people whose ideas of spiritual evolution were far
in advance of anything else around in those early days and they
may not have truly understood what they were taught, but at
least they tried. Their teachers, it would appear, conceived of an
evolved state into which everything was ultimately absorbed, be
it animal, vegetable or mineral; nor were they conceited enough
to view this state of 'god' as being in their own image and
likeness only.

A whole universe existed beyond Earth, a universe which
could house 'god' in an infinite number of manifestations, some
of which could assume a physical likeness and some that were
purely abstract. After all, why should any deity look like *Homo
sapiens*? To a race of people possessing knowledge of other life
forms beyond Earth this idea would have seemed ridiculous and
the concept of the existence of a single intelligence at the point of
creation also highly illogical. If all created 'sparks' ultimately
homed in on or returned to their creator, taking with them the
knowledge gained by journeying through many time zones
(other lives, for those who see time as linear), they would hardly
become lost as individualities but would surely continue to exist
as aspects, fragments, or even personifications of the whole. If
everything evolves to that point, as the Egyptians believed, then
why not a cat, cow, tree or star as representations of the
ultimate? We all need terms of reference and to those who, upon
reading this, throw up their hands in holy horror and cry
'blasphemy' I would say, 'You are the blasphemers even to
consider anything that is the work of the Creator as unworthy of
his name or representation.'

The inner mysteries of the Egyptian temples were by no
means as polytheistic as might be imagined. It was generally
believed that certain aspects of the deity, or 'sons and daughters
of god', were responsible for this planet and all things that
thrived thereon. The idea of a trinity appealed to them, but in a
more solid and less prejudiced form than the father/son/bird
symbolism of Christianity. Polarities they saw as being logical

and practical, and the normal outcome of such a fusing was a third energy, personified as a son or daughter.

So it was not so much the cat, dog or snake that was worshipped, but the principle it represented; and that principle was, in turn, an aspect of the greater creation or ultimate spirit. The priesthood was well aware of all this, but found it expedient to incorporate local nature deities into advanced spiritual concepts, as well as allowing people to make their own 'god pictures', as it didn't really matter how the detail was expressed as long as the ethic was observed and the spiritual needs catered for. People, in the final analysis, usually find their own level, so religious prejudice of any sort is futile and can only lead to anguish and suffering (as may be witnessed throughout the pages of history).

A better understanding of the true nature of the Egyptian religion has been propounded by later scholars whose writings and dialogues we shall examine, but before embarking upon a consideration of the deeper philosophy it might be advisable to see if there is a line of demarcation between theological concepts, as personified, and actual people, teachers, doctors, rulers etc., who later appeared in deified form.

From myth and legend there would seem to be ample evidence to support the theory that Isis and her family were actual people, perhaps from Atlantis or some other advanced civilization, or even from some distant star system. Thoth/ Tehuti, or even Imhotep, may have been their physician, and amongst their band there could have been 'aliens' of another species, maybe resembling cats, lions, or what have you. Or these people may have trained animals to a high degree, so that they were not fierce and primitive but useful and more kindly disposed towards man. An open mind is an essential prerequisite for the aspiring magician.

Equally worthy of consideration is the idea that Isis and her family represented a parable of an actual cosmic event, such as a shift in the Earth's axis, a change in the position of the Moon, and astronomical events witnessed by a technologically advanced race who had no other means of communicating their knowledge to a primitive people. In other words, the whole thing could have a sound scientific basis and, in view of recent scientific discoveries in the field of quantum mechanics, this is all highly feasible. It is known that sub-atomic particles can communicate instantaneously with one another over vast distances of outer space, so why can't human minds do the same thing? There would appear to be nothing new on Earth, only things forgotten.

From the standpoint of magic, the Egyptian system does request of its followers that they relate to a clearly defined adherence where the gods are concerned, so the student should be definite about his initial choice. I shall outline the one I have found to be the most efficacious and best suited to modern conditions and requirements. Magic asks for an acknowledgement of the existence of forces beyond the normal energies that are visible and negotiable in day-to-day living. If you don't believe in these in the first place, you are wasting your time studying magic of any kind. Mind you, as has already been stated, believing or not believing makes no difference to the nature and power of a force or energy field. After all, the Elizabethans didn't believe in electricity, but electricity was still there. Scientists earlier this century would have dismissed theories about atomic energy as science fiction, pie in the sky, or simply heretical; and yet it existed in spite of their protests.

The nature of space-time is still being hotly debated, but many an occultist knows that all time exists simultaneously and that ultimately there will be a technology to prove this and to negotiate the time barrier as easily as we now catch a jet to the other side of the globe. It is my personal opinion that the people who taught the early Egyptians knew many of these things and we are about to complete the circle of knowledge at any moment now.

This will call for a new look at old theologies in the cosmic light of a combined scientific logic and spiritual understanding. Magical principles are constant throughout the universe; only the names affixed to them in each epoch of time differ. If we are to weather the storm of religious confusion and uncertainty that will doubtless be created by the oncoming tide of scientific revelation, we must prepare ourselves mentally by considering the deeper aspects of the universe in the light of knowledge. There is *no dividing line*. Science and the occult are not the two opposing forces they are made out to be; in fact, they are closer allies than faith and orthodoxy.

Once science has established an acceptable set of terms of reference for what has loosely been termed 'magic' in the past, the superstition will fall away and the gods of ancient Egypt will assume a new role in the inter-cosmic scheme of things.

6. PYRAMID POWER

The pyramids have been a very popular topic for observation, debate and investigation over the past few years. Endless books have appeared covering the mathematics of these super-structures, the reason for their erection in the first place, their occult significance and their defiance of the laws of modern science. It has been postulated that they were built by some anti-gravitational force, sonics, spacemen, telekinesis or, last but not least, by hordes of poor little slaves hauling large slabs of stones up inclined ramps.

That there is some connection between the pyramidal structures and the history and evolution of our planet has become increasingly obvious of late. For example, the basic unit of measurement that the designer appears to have used turns out to be an exact ten-millionth of the Earth's polar radius; and this is only one of many similarly related mathematical 'coincidences'. Decoding the message of the Great Pyramid has become a popular pastime among authors with the mathematical know-how, leaving the reader with numerous theories to choose from. We are told that the sacred number associated with this pyramid is five. In Egyptian magic this is Thoth's number, on the one hand, and the magical number for Sirius on the other.

Even from a purely materialistic and scientific standpoint there would appear to be more to the pyramids than meets the eye. For example, a project was set up recently by the United

Arab Republic and the United States to X-ray the Chephren pyramid in search of some hitherto undiscovered burial chamber. Normal X-rays not being considered powerful enough to penetrate the stonework, Dr Luis Alvarez, a Nobel prizewinner for physics and director of the Lawrence Radiation Laboratory at the University of California, suggested his equipment might fit the bill. This technology was developed to measure the radiation particles bombarding the Earth from outer space, so it was logically assumed that, if it were placed in the existing burial chamber in Chephren's pyramid, the amount of radiation reaching the chamber through the stonework could be recorded on tape and any deviation in the solidity of the structure could be noted. This would make it comparatively easy to trace any additional burial chambers that had not, as yet, come to light.

The complicated radiation apparatus, operating at some 10,000 volts, was duly installed and a considerable amount of cosmic ray information collected as a result; there was certainly enough to answer the original query. Lauren Yazolino of California University stated, 'We have run two tapes through the computer and are satisfied that our equipment is functioning correctly.' Dr Alvarez visited the pyramid to collect the recorded tapes from his apparatus and then promptly left without making any comment on his findings. Dr Amir Gohed, of El Shams University, Cairo, was left in charge of the equipment once the Americans had left and his only significant comment was, 'It defies all the known laws of science and electronics; in fact, the taped results are scientifically impossible. The tapes we had hoped would reveal a great discovery are a jumbled mass of meaningless symbols. Two tapes which should be exactly the same are totally different. Either the geometry of the pyramid is substantially erroneous, which we know it is not, or there is a mystery which is beyond explanation. Call it what you will – occultism, the curse of the pharaohs, sorcery or magic – there is some force at work in Chephren's pyramid that defies all the known laws of science.'

The pyramids have certainly managed to hold their secret, but for how much longer? Will science eventually come up with the correct answer? I am personally of the opinion that it will and am therefore happy to wait until that time. But this does not prevent me, or any other student of Egyptian magic, from tossing around a few ideas based, perhaps, on more meta-physical observations.

It has been postulated that the shape and structure of the pyramids is in some unfathomable way capable of slowing down the normal processes of decay. Experimenters have had a whale of a time with razor blades and foodstuffs which, we are informed, do appear to enjoy longer life spans when subjected to periods of time within scale models of the Great Pyramid. The preserving qualities of this sacred geometry were obviously only partly understood by the Egyptians, who tended to use them as tombs in which to place their mummified corpses in the pious hope of preserving the bodies for re-use in some more exalted dimension.

But, from an occult standpoint, is there anything in all this? A few years back I was a lecturer at a leading esoteric conference in England where a society specializing in pyramidology set up a scale model pyramid that would accommodate a man in a meditative posture. A well-known swami of great repute agreed to try it out and, after about ten minutes, he emerged with a very perplexed look on his face. I asked him what happened. 'I'd rather not comment immediately,' he told me, but invited me to try and see what I felt. I received my impressions in con-siderably less than ten minutes and related them to the swami. We had both experienced exactly the same thing: a suspension of time, as though moving to a point where several time zones merged.

When the human brain is not programmed to compute multi-time synchronies the result of being exposed to such a phenomenon is baffling, to say the least. But it would appear that we do possess the necessary mechanisms in our brain structures to handle enlightenment of this sort and it is only a question of time and patience before they are accepted as the norm by our rational thinking mind. According to psychic sources, evolutionary quantum leaps are supposed to occur at intervals involving thousands of years and, at these times, areas of the human brain, hitherto unexercised, will become active and proceed to decode what were formerly mysteries or science fiction fantasies.

Thinking about the pyramids also tunes me into my old theme that the early Egyptians simply produced replicas of what they had observed among the technological achievements of their 'visitors', without fully understanding the implications of such handiwork. History tells us that the main pyramids were originally coated with an outer substance, possibly marble, and furnished with metal-covered cones or capstones. Their angle in relation to the Earth's axis and the solar path is also worth studying, but these considerations would take up a book in themselves and there is already plenty of this type of research literature about.

Your author is constantly being asked whether she has spent a lone night in a pyramid. The answer is no, not in the body. But as space and time are irrelevant to occult and magical development, then the question should be rephrased to enquire whether she is familiar with the initiatory rites of the pyramids, the answer to which would be in the affirmative.

Pyramid initiation predates Egypt and is based on the principle that, at a certain stage in the development of the aspiring magus, it becomes necessary for him or her to understand the nature of time and negotiate multi-time dimensions. In other words, one gets one's ticket to the universe, take it or leave it. Tradition has it that when the initiates were placed in the pyramid and sealed in for three days and three nights, if they emerged sane they were worthy of the mantle of the true priesthood. But, if they failed, they were either dead when the seals were broken or brought forth as mental vegetables.

The initiation of the pyramid can be undertaken in the etheric state, i.e., on projection, and the first picture usually encountered is of the original structures from which the existing edifices were copied. These had metal cones containing time-projector mechanisms, the co-ordinates of which were astronomically aligned to specific stellar points. Of course, the spirit does not rely upon the encumbrances of technological paraphernalia to aid it in its flight out into the universe as this can be achieved by pure mind. But, at some time in the distant past, it would seem that there were actual physical journeys undertaken by a people who could negotiate the space-time field, using a state of temporary time-suspension as a kick-off.

Much of initiation is involved with learning how to cope with new states of awareness, or ASCs (altered states of consciousness), and balancing acquired knowledge against the order and rationale of everyday human existence within a single linear time dimension. It is not surprising, therefore, that for some aspirants the effect of this sort of exposure proves too mind-blowing to cope with and, to use a computer term, they 'loop'. It happens all the time to people who insist upon embarking on the magical path when they are emotionally and psychologically totally unsuited to it. 'Man, know thyself' and all that.

When several time zones are condensed into a single picture, as takes place during pyramidal initiation, a withdrawal from the enclosure of this present Earth time zone is called for. Vast epochs of time, covering millions and billions of years as we would understand time, are encapsulated in a single visionary experience for which there are no available terms of reference, and all one can say is 'you will see what I mean if and when you come up against it'. Science handles it all much better than the human mind at present, as quantum physics can present the entire picture in a neatly arranged equation. Using one's creative imagination to relate pictorially to a mathematical equation can be mind blowing for some people, but for the initiate who has emerged from the pyramidal journey there would be no problems.

If we, the human species, are to evolve in a balanced way, it is important that our technological achievements do not outstrip the rate of our mental and spiritual growth. In other words, we must spiritually understand what is being fed to us at the material level and, if we do not, that gap will become a void and produce psychological alienations on a scale envisaged by many a science fiction writer. So, as our dear white-coated friends slowly unravel the secrets of the mechanical (and now unseen) universe, it is the task of the time-travelled souls among us to keep mental pace and act as spiritual translators for those younger souls who might find the crumbling of their religious edifices too much to take.

When writing about practical Egyptian magic, in a later chapter, I shall outline some safe techniques for dealing with the pyramidal shapes and coming to comfortable terms with 'outer time' and all that it implies.

There have been many 'suggestions' received from psychic sources regarding both the pyramids and the sphinx. One of the most popular is concerned with the climate in Egypt at the time when these structures were raised. As we have already seen, in the earliest Recension of *The Book of the Dead*, there are comments to the effect that the land we now see as hot, desertlike, and watered by the Nile, was not always that way. Much of the Sahara was a sea in time long gone, and the sphinx is reputed to have been erected during a period of high vegetation and verdant landscapes. One legend even has it that it stands on a pillar and that there is a hidden chamber, or temple, somewhere far beneath. During a movement in the Earth's axis the climate altered drastically and the sands covered the base.

It is up to each individual to choose what to believe about the sphinx and the pyramids. Perhaps, after you have practised Egyptian magic for a while, assuming that you take to it or that it takes to you, you will no doubt formulate your own ideas as to the whys and wherefores of this ancient monument to time and human evolution and, for my part, that is about as much as I intend to say on the subject.

Magic is a journey of discovery for the brave and stable individual and, as with any dangerous journey, we do not deny that there are dangers to be encountered along the path. Discovering cosmic truths for oneself can open up a world of wonderment and no teacher has the right to deny the pupil this experience. But, just as you would not consider embarking on a climb of Everest wearing only shorts, a T-shirt and flip-flaps, it is not advisable to step forth onto the path of magical conquest armed only with curiosity and an outsized ego. The path of magical initiation calls for the journeying spirit to be armed with the stability and practicality of the elements of earth (gnomes); the loyalty, ardour and creativity of the elements of fire (salamanders); the mental speed, communication and inventiveness of the elements of air (sylphs) and the receptivity, understanding and adaptability of the water elements (ondines). In other words, man needs his fourfold nature fully verified and readily available in emergency because as sure as eggs are eggs, whether you are in or out of a pyramid, you are going to need it.

7. TOMBS AND CURSES

Many people I have encountered, who consider themselves rather a spiritual cut above others, tend to look down on the ancient Egyptian priesthood because of the use of 'protectors' on their tombs or holy places. When happily chatting to a vicar a year or so ago I remarked on this fact and he laughingly replied, 'I wish I could muster up a few ghoulies to frighten away the hooligans who are constantly pinching the lead off my church roof.' Obviously not a spiritual snob, but a very practical man.

The ethical question inevitably arises, should one conjure forth something to do one's bidding and, assuming one possesses the know-how to do this, should the poor creature be encapsulated in a time zone from which it cannot escape without the aid of a magician of equal power to the original spell binder?

Who are we in our glasshouses to throw stones at those Egyptian priests who earnestly believed it was their duty to protect both the bodies and souls, or spirits, of those who placed themselves in their sacerdotal care? But there are, perhaps, kinder ways of going about things, as we shall shortly see.

The main methods of tomb protection employed by the Egyptian priests fell into two categories, the evocation of elemental spirits (spirits of the elements and *not* prehuman-type energies) and the creation of artificial elementals or ensouled thought forms. (See my book *Practical Techniques of Psychic Self-Defence.*) The earlier Egyptian occult practitioners favoured the four elements as defenders against tomb violation, but in the Middle Kingdom the thought form method was in vogue, probably because the priests of Amen were not on very understanding terms with our fourfold friends. Stories of genii imprisoned in bottles hold more than a grain of truth, as the ancient magi knew the art of luring a single element from its group soul and encapsulating it in some object or confined space. By the occult law of equalities only a magician of equal or greater power may release the poor thing but, as time is irrelevant to elemental spirits, it's all rather academic. Or is it?

Fire elementals, or salamanders, were favourites with the Egyptian priest for guarding tombs, which is why so many molesters of sacred Egyptian places met with fiery ends or violent accidents. At this point I must make it quite clear that salamanders are *not* killers. They were simply programmed to function according to the law of rebound which dictates that, if anyone is foolish enough to break into a place protected by a salamander, that fire energy will thenceforth attach itself to the offender. What causes the death is usually the inability of the new host to accommodate its fiery companion; i.e., it mentally unbalances him so that he drives wildly, becomes overheated physically, or finds himself drawn towards fiery places or objects, which is simply the poor old salamander trying to get back home.

The wise magician who has recourse to the favours of an elemental should always issue it with instructions to depart when the task is completed, so that it is not trapped in any time dimension. Elements called during occult workings should be dismissed to the four corners of the compass with which they are associated, i.e., fire to the south, earth to the north, air to the east and water to the west. The ancient Egyptians had their faults (don't we all?), one of which was that they tended not to think things through. They were playing with magic wands inherited from people who were more familiar with the universe, so can we really blame them?

The other method used for guarding tombs was the creation of artificial elementals or ensouled thought forms. The *modus operandi* for creating and ensouling thought forms simply involves attracting or generating subtle energies, which are then fashioned into entity form and endowed with individual qualities; or, alternatively, encouraging some other discarnate spirit or alien intelligence to utilize the power on a temporary basis. In my humble opinion the creation of 'artificial elementals' is unethical and there is no reason whatsoever for employing it. If you have reached the standard of occult development necessary for evocation you will be able to *request*, in humility, the aid of the elemental kingdoms. If you haven't arrived at that point in your initiations you will only create havoc and chaos in somebody else's life (or your own, for that matter) through dabbling with powers that are beyond you.

Protection can be effected against magical spells that have been placed on Egyptian tombs, but only in accordance with the law of equalities. This means that anything of equal power can be coped with but, if the originating magus was of greater occult prowess, the challenger must either stand down or be forced down by the energies encountered. When several persons are present during the opening of a tomb it is logical to assume that some must be of lesser occult power than the priests who placed the protection thereon. (I don't like the word 'curse'; after all, they didn't curse anyone in particular and usually only asked the force evoked to deal with intruders or 'nasties'.) This is why there have been instances where certain men escaped unharmed while others met with peculiar and tragic ends following research programmes on sepulchres.

If one really wants to poke about amongst places that could well have been protected by the magi of old, the best thing to do is to engage an occultist in one's party to take care of any such contingencies, preferably one versed in the Egyptian arts. Being a believer in another religion, no matter how large the membership of that faith may be, is no protection against the forces of Egyptian magic.

The ancient Egyptians were taught by a people who were strictly schooled in the ethics of universal occultism, a system of magic that is unique unto itself. Its powers can only be effectively controlled through the manipulation of certain basic cosmic laws and not through the intercession of emotionally generated or illogically orientated Earth faiths. I had several small Ushapti from a very famous 'dig' and on one occasion I loaned one of these to a gentleman friend. He literally threw it back at me after a few days, declaring that it moved about on his pillow and floated above him of its own volition. He was a devout Christian, but all his entreaties to the Almighty failed to make the thing lie down. It now resides happily round the neck of another gentleman who is completely in accord with it, as I am myself.

Coming back to our tomb guardians, protections can be effected by magical means without having recourse to drastic measures. One doesn't need a sledgehammer to crack a nut. Besides, once activated, artificial entities can be difficult to dissolve if their originator dies or loses contact, causing something of a problem for others to cope with. As time does not exist in the next dimension, a thought form once created can exist for centuries in Earth time and prove a thorough nuisance until some powerful practitioner comes face to face with it and releases it. I refer here to the encapsulation of an actual spirit within a falsely created energy field and not necessarily to a thought form that has been generated simply by someone thinking a life into it from his or her own personal psyche. Fire elementals do not much care for being stuck around Egyptian tombs, or being corked into bottles, come to that, and are usually eternally grateful to their liberator. In fact, they will hang about and try to do all sorts of 'favours', so the best way of dealing with the situation is to dismiss them, with love and thanks, to their own group element, from which they may individualize in their own evolutionary time. Working with elemental spirits of this kind does, however, speed up their development as they learn a lot from humans, just as we learn from them.

The Egyptian priests of the Middle Kingdom worked a rather different system of magic from those of earlier times. As with any seeker after truth who becomes too involved in temporal powers, their ability to negotiate the finer spiritual realms was sadly diminished. Much was done to rectify this during the Saite Recension of *The Book of the Dead* and it is to those industrious scribes that we owe much of the knowledge of earlier Egyptian esoteric beliefs and practices that has come through to us today.

Before embarking upon any magical exercises the Egyptian student was always taught what were broadly termed the 'mysteries'. Many of these Egyptian 'mysteries' were passed down by word of mouth, secret occult teaching and tradition over the centuries. We are indebted to several later writers and scholars for the information now to hand, which stands head and shoulders above more recent faiths, especially when viewed in the light of new age scientific discoveries and 'thinking'. Our circle is slowly closing, and the symbolism of the ouroboros (serpent eating its own tail) becomes more and more obvious.

Was he one or many, merging
   Name and fame in one,
Like a stream, to which, converging,
   Many streamlets run?

●　　●　　●

Who shall call his dreams fallacious?
   Who has searched or sought
All the unexplored and spacious
   Universe of thought?

Who in his own skill confiding,
   Shall with rule and line
Mark the border-land dividing
   Human and divine?

Trismegistus! Three times greatest!
   How thy name sublime
Has descended to this latest
   Progeny of time!

Hermes Trismegistus
Longfellow

8. THE HERMES TRIGMEGISTUS

Part I: Sources

For the modern student of Egyptian belief and thought, the bible or main book of reference is undoubtedly the *Hermes Trismegistus* or *Thrice Greatest Hermes*. Its writings were said to have been inspired by Thoth/Tehuti himself, just as the Christians declare that their sacred writings were checked out by the Holy Spirit. My own three volumes of the *Hermes* were catalogued by the theosophical scholar G.R.S. Mead at the end of the last century; it is to these and the Iamblichos/Porphyry dialogues which appear under the title of *The Egyptian Mysteries* that many present day followers of Egyptian magic owe much of their learning.

Why 'thrice greatest Hermes'? There are several explanations, one being that this literature is closely allied to Hermetic masonry, a secret cult which flourished in Europe in the eighteenth century and was, in turn, a rehashed version of an earlier mystery school, possibly Templarism. The law of three requests, an occult law requiring that any deeply significant magical request must be presented three times, was usually strictly adhered to in this discipline. The principle behind this law is that at the first declaration the conscious mind is alerted, at the second the subconscious is brought into play and, at the third, the spirit is sufficiently in communication with both levels of consciousness to be able to answer for itself without interference from the programmed rationale or metaphysical inclinations in popular vogue. A classic example of this is the biblical request made by Jesus to Peter, which was repeated thrice.

Another interpretation of the 'thrice greatest' tag is the significance of the numerology of the 'three' in its expansive and educative mode.

The *Trismegistus* represents part of a collection of ancient Egyptian occult teachings which are distinguished from the 'Hermes prayers' of Egyptian magic and the Hermetic alchemical literature. In fact, they stand alone. They comprise:

(a) The Corpus Hermeticum (body of the teachings), which includes The Poimandres, a collection of fourteen sermons, and The Definitions of Asclepius involving instructions from Hermes to the said Greek healer.

(b) The Perfect Sermon, also known as the Asclepius as it is addressed to a character of that name. This exists only in the old Latin version, the Greek now being extinct.

(c) The Excerpts from Stobaeus. There are twenty-seven of these excerpts from otherwise lost sermons that were 'found' and re-translated by one John Stobaeus, a pagan scholar from the end of the fifth and beginning of the sixth centuries. Stobaeus collected extracts, some of which are very long, especially the collection entitled *The Virgin of the World,* from the Greek authors and occult schools of his day. In your author's opinion this one is among the best of the twenty-seven excerpts appearing in the form of a series of instructions from Isis to her son, Horus, in the art of Egyptian magic and the Egyptian mysteries.

(d) The references and fragments from the early Christian fathers. The early Christian scholars and Church doctors frequently commented on the *Hermes Trismegistus* and there are twenty-five short fragments of note that have come down to us. Because of the heretical nature of the Hermetic doctrine these writers tended to speak out against it, which very act has, in fact, helped to keep it alive. It is interesting to note, however, that in spite of their opposition, they definitely convey an underlying acknowledgement of, if not an actual respect for, the Trismegistic power and philosophy.

(e) References and fragments from the early philosophers, not necessarily Christian. From Zosimus, Fulgentius and Iamblichus we obtain three fragments and from Julian, the emperor philosopher (irreverently labelled 'the apostate' by his Christian contemporaries), there are a number of valuable references and acknowledgements.

The testimony afforded by these historical passages accords with much of what has come down to us from verbal traditional sources, inner lodge instructions from master to pupil, and mystical inspiration. Errors have obviously crept in, with translators tending to re-interpret the texts in the light of both their own experiences and current trends of occultism´fashionable during their lifetime. These fragments are but the scant remains of what must once have been an abundant literature largely reserved for the dedicated student or initiate, much of which would have been entirely lost were it not for the diligent efforts of one Hermetic apologist selecting some of the sermons to exemplify the loyal nature of the *Hermes Trismegistus* with respect to the position of kings.

The fact that these fragmentary odds and ends have somehow managed to straddle the centuries, in spite of severe mutilation resulting from translation and re-translation, is a miracle in itself. At times they existed purely as secret works when persecution was rife; at other periods they remained safely in the possession of private collectors or 'guardians' of the word. But in spite of all the opposition from unfriendly sources, both incarnate and discarnate, a few gems from the old truths have managed to filter through to us.

An index of full references would take up too much space and is not really relevant to Egyptian magic, but for the benefit of the dedicated researcher I will list a few verifiable sources. Embodying the Hellenic and Orphic tradition as related to the *Hermes Trismegistus* there is the *Bibliotheca Graeca* of Joannes Albertus Fabricius (fourth and last edition, Leipzig, 1790). From alchemical and medieval literature we have the works of M.P.E. Berthelot, namely: *Collection des Anciens Alchimistes Grecs* (Paris 1888) and *La Chimie au Moyen Age* (Paris 1893). Arabic writings include Beausobre's *Histoire Critique de Manichée et du Manichéism* i. 326 (Amsterdam 1734); also H.L. Fleischer, *Hermes Trismegistus an die Menschlibche Seele, Arabisch und Deutsch* (Leipzig 1870); O. Bardenhewer, *Hermetis Trismegisti qui apud Arabes fertur de Castigatione Animae Liber* (Bon 1873); and Pietschmann, the pupil of Georg

Ebers, who devoted the fourth part of his treatise entitled *Hermes Trismegistus nach agyptischen und orientalischen Uberlieferungen* (Leipzig 1875) to a consideration of the Hermes tradition.

Another single manuscript was found in the eleventh century in sad condition. Whole quires and single leaves were missing when it came into the hands of one Michael Psellus, a gentleman greatly involved in the revival of Platonic studies at Byzantium. Sadly, though, large chunks of this Psellus translation were torn out because they sought directly to justify polytheism or 'heathendom', so once again the serious student was cheated. The theosophical scholar Reitzenstein did as much as he could to piece together the fragments of truth and Mead speaks highly of his efforts.

Much of the Trismegistic literature is taken from original Greek texts, although there were three influences superimposed on the early originals later, Greek, Hebrew and Egyptian. The Jewish influence was Essenic or Therapeutic (the word Essene is, Mead tells us, Greek and not Hebrew). The *Trismegistus*, then, came under the influence of the early Christian Gnostics, many of whom adopted large chunks of it in defence of their 'heresies'. The most notable of these was Basilides, whom the great psychologist Carl Jung believed to be either a fragment of his own group soul guiding him in trance through the *Seven Sermons of the Dead*, or himself in a former life. The Valentinian Gnosis was also strongly Hermetical. The Gnostic flavour in the Trismegistus literature is therefore obviously very strong, so it will pay the student to strip away some of these Christo-Gnostic overleaves in order to get a little nearer to the Egyptian original.

The whole series which comprise the *Trismegistus* is attributed to the direct inspiration of Hermes, the Greek Thoth/ Tehuti, who is referred to as 'the master of wisdom and teacher of mankind'. The *Trismegistus* tells us that Thoth 'ordained measure, number and order in the universe; was master architect (hence Hermetic masonry), and his wife or consort was Nehemaut, known to the Gnostics as Sophia and as Maat to the Egyptians. His symbol was a white feather and all his other qualifications are exactly as I have already enumerated under his heading as an Egyptian god of great antiquity.

According to the *Hermes Trismegistus* there were three grades in the Egyptian mysteries of Thoth:

Mortals. Those who were instructed but who had not yet gained inner vision.

Intelligences. Those whose vision enabled them to tune into other life forms within the universe.

Beings of light. Those who had become one with the light.

The Gnostics later labelled these as the hyle, psyche and pneuma.

Thoth's famous ibis often comes under astrological scrutiny and there has been much debate as to which sign it represents. As the Zodiac was originally known as 'the circle of animals' one should not assume that the human signs we now see as the water carrier, the twins and the virgin were originally depicted thus. As divine teacher and Akashic librarian Thoth has, by nature, a lot in common with Virgo, but Aquarius has also been seen to suit his nature on account of the 'waters of knowledge' that the bearer pours forth on mankind, and Libra as representing his heavenly judicial status.

In Gnostic literature Thoth is the tutor to both Isis and Osiris and is one of the sacred 'eight', four pairs of divinities each a syzygy of male and female powers, positive and negative, active and passive, which is the oldest example of the Gnostic Ogdoad. Thoth's job, the *Hermes Trismegistus* informs us, is to keep perfect equipoise; hence his main symbol, the caduceus.

In order to understand Egyptian magic fully, and therefore become adept at its practice, a broad knowledge of the symbolism employed is essential. Some Gnostic/Egyptian symbols can cause confusion, but only if one has not actually practised Egyptian magic. The girdle of Aphrodite, for example, which is also part of Greek magic, becomes associated with both Thoth and Ptah in the Hermetic system with obvious masonic implications. As lord of karma, Thoth was granted the power to bind or loose, hence his connection; whereas in Greek magic Aphrodite's girdle is a protective symbol as representing the only force (love) that can withstand the thunderbolts of Zeus by averting them. If Zeus took it into his head to hurl a thunderbolt at someone the poor offender was totally without protection, unless he or she could court the good offices of the goddess of love who might then see fit to interpose with her girdle; indications, and clear ones, of love being the most powerful force in the universe in the final analysis.

Another symbol that appears in the Egyptian Hermetic

system that has Hellenistic overtones is the veil of Athene, goddess of wisdom. This is a spiritual veil and not synonymous with the 'veil' lifted by the earnest seeker of truth who has just discovered the halls of learning. Also, it should not be confused with the shield of Athene or her famous helmet, both potent symbols in the Greek system.

In the *Book of Breathings* Thoth is referred to as 'master of the breath of the body and control over the physical vehicle', so his association with mantra yoga is an obvious one. He is depicted as attended by Anubis, which gives him safe right of way through the underworld or lower astral.

The devic nature of Thoth/Hermes is confirmed in several prayers set forth in the *Trismegistus*: 'Enter, appear to me, O lord, who has thy power and strength in fire, who hast thy throne within the seven poles. And on thy head a golden crown, and in thy hand a staff, by which thou sendest forth the gods.' (The rod of power which directs the 'gods', or seven rays of manifestations of the Sun.) The Greek influence is obvious here, but this should not, and indeed does not, affect the efficacy of the Egyptian magical system as taught in these works.

Greek philosophy and Egyptian lore really came together at the time of the Lagides, who gradually made Alexandria the intellectual, scientific, philosophic and religious centre of the Hellenistic world. In fact, the clear thinking of Greek logic served to peel away quite a few of the outer layers that had accumulated in the Egyptian system over the centuries, bringing it much nearer to the original than, say, the occultism of the Theban or middle period. Manetho, the Egyptian priest of Heliopolis, was also famous for translating the mysteries into Greek. He lived during the final years of the fourth and first half of the third centuries B.C. in the reign of the last two Ptolemies.

As far as this enquiry is concerned, one fragment of writing that has come down to us is of considerable importance and we owe its preservation to one Georgius Syncellus. It is stated to be taken from a work of Manetho, entitled *Sothis*, that has otherwise entirely disappeared. The passage with the introductory sentence of the monk Syncellus runs as follows:

It is proposed then to make a few extracts concerning the Egyptian dynasties from the Books of Manetho (this Manetho) being High Priest of the Heathen Temples in Egypt, based his replies (to King

Ptolemy) on the monuments which lay in the Seriadic country. (These monuments) he tells us, were engraved in the sacred language and in the characters of the sacred writing by Thoth, the first Hermes; after the Flood they were translated from the sacred language into the then common tongue, but (still written) in hieroglyphic characters, and stored away in books by the Good Daimons and the second Hermes, father of Tat, in the inner chambers of the Temples of Egypt.

There is a lot more in this document and for those interested I would recommend the Mead translation; the references to a land of enlightened people that existed before the flood, and to the fact that Thoth/Hermes and the other 'gods' came from such a country, are numerous and leave little doubt in any open mind as to where the Egyptians gained their occult knowledge. It is interesting, also, to note that the old truths were translated from the tongue of the mother country into the native Egyptian and no doubt suffered not only in translation but in subsequent analysis by later generations of scholars to whom the whole pre-flood story was little more than an historical fable. Sothis is another name for Sirius, which brings us to the next piece of information from this stable.

References to 'the Seriadic land' have confused more conventionally inclined scholars who claim that there is no historical record of a Seriadic land or country. Mead states, 'In the astronomical science of the Egyptians, the most conspicuous solar system near our own, represented in the heavens by the brilliant Sirius, was of supreme interest. Cycles of immense importance were determined by it, and it entered into the highest mysticism of Egyptian initiation.' Sirius was the guardian star of Egypt, its rising greatly affecting the life of everyday folk through the yearly inundation from the Nile. As the basis of this cycle of inundation was Sothiac or Syriadic, Sirius (Seirios) being called in the Greek transliteration Sothis and Seth (e.g., Sept), it surely stands to reason that Egypt was 'the Seriadic land'.

In antiquity there were constant references to the 'pillars of Hermes', or 'Mercurii columnae', from which many of the ancient writers claim to have gathered their information. The historian Ammianus Marcellinus, friend of the Emperor Julian, has preserved some information which is certainly of interest. It runs as follows:

There are certain underground galleries and passages full of windings, which, it is said, the adepts in the ancient rites (knowing that the flood was coming, and fearing that the memory of the sacred ceremonies would be obliterated) constructed in various places, distributed in the interior (of the buildings), which were mined out with great labour. And levelling the walls, they engraved on them numerous kinds of birds and animals, and countless varieties (of creatures) of another world, which they called hieroglyphic characters.

A highly significant passage from the Hermetic texts appears in the writings of one Sanchuniathon, who is described by Philo as 'a man of great learning and a busy searcher (after knowledge) who especially desired to know the first principles from which all things are derived ...' Philo continues to inform us that Sanchuniathon 'most carefully examined the books of Taaut, for he knew that Taaut was the first of all under the sun who discovered the use of letters and the writing of records. So he started from him, making him as it were his foundation, from him the Logos whom the Egyptians call Thouth, the Alexandrians Thoth, but whom the Greeks have turned into Hermes.' The paragraphs relating to the creation are of particular interest and far removed from the primitive thinking normally associated with other indigenous peoples of the African continent. I feel they are worthy of detailed quotation:

He (Thoth) supposes the beginning of all things to consist of a Dark Mist of a spiritual nature, or as it were a Breath of dark mist, and of a turbid Chaos black as Erebus; that these were boundless, and for many an age remained without a bound. 'But when,' he says, 'the spirit fell in love with its own principles, and they were interblended, that interweaving was called Love; and this Love was the origin of the creation of all things. But (Chaos) did not know its own creation. From its embrace with Spirit Mot was born. From her (Mot, the Great Mother) it was that every seed of the creation came, the birth of all the cosmic bodies.

(First of all) there were (Great) Lives devoid of sensation, and out of these came subsequently (Great) Lives possessed of intelligence. The latter were called Zophasemin (that is to say, "Overseers of the Heavens"). The latter were fashioned in the form of eggs, and shone forth as Mot, the Sun and Moon, the Stars and the great Planetary Spheres.

Now as the (original) nebula began to lighten, through its heat mists and clouds of sea and earth were produced, and gigantic downpours and torrents of the waters in the firmaments. Even after they were separated, they were still carried from their proper places by the heat of the sun, and all the (watery and earthy elements) met together again in the nebula one with the other, and dashed together, amid thunder and lightning; and over the crash of the thunderings the (Great) Rational Lives before-mentioned watched, while on the land and sea male and female cowered at their echo and were dismayed . . .'

A considerable knowledge of cosmology and the Earth's early evolutionary cycle is indicated in these passages, and there is plenty more. In fact, these Egyptian 'mysteries' have far more in common with modern scientific trends of thinking than many an orthodox faith generally accepted by the mass of people in our so-called 'enlightened' age.

As has already been commented, many of the early Christian scholars opposed the Trismegistic literature and did everything in their power either to suppress or ridicule it. Hippolytus and the famous anti-reincarnationalist, Irenaeus of Gaul, did their fair share of knocking the old truths, and a French expedition rediscovered a few of these writings in a monastery on Mount Athos in 1842. It is a great pity that these early fathers came to label any form of magic or occultism as heretical and, because certain Gnostic heretics of the period, probably the Naasenes and Ophites, embraced Egyptian principles amongst their general hotch-potch of pseudo-Christian and Hellenistic inclinations, the baby was well and truly cast forth with its proverbial bath water. The Naasenes (from the word Nahash, serpent) incidentally were responsible for translating a document telling of a city of four rivers that existed centuries earlier where Hermes himself originally dwelt. Not programmed to consider civilizations earlier than Egypt, the Gnostics related the four rivers to aspects of the mind. We are, however, grateful to them and to the early Christian scholars for their translations and acknowledgements, even if we do not approve of their bigoted and irrational arguments.

9. THE HERMES TRISMEGISTUS

Part II: The Teachings

The Trismegistic literature is a study in itself and to cover all the points contained therein salient to Egyptian magic would prove too lengthy a process. There are, however, some facets of these fragments highly relevant to the subject, without which knowledge the progress of the neophyte could be hindered if not actually curtailed. Take the nature of Osiris, for example. Osiris, according to Hermes Trismegistus, was a water divinity, more Dionysiac than Poseidonian. It is interesting to note that in old Egyptian art work he is usually depicted as seated on a throne surrounded by water. From this water a lotus has emerged, within whose petals are seated the four sons of Horus. Mead tells us that the name Osiris actually means 'moist' and, when invoking Osiris at the Elysinia, the priests used to cry 'hye kye' meaning 'oh moistener beget'. This was not a fertility rite, incidentally, the 'begettings' having other connotations. Osiris was said to possess a heavenly drinking horn or chalice that never ran dry, rather after the style of the cauldron of Dagda in the Irish Celtic cycle. Another symbol of his (as with Dionysus) was the ship, or sacred barque, sometimes called 'the ship of the dead'. During initiation this symbol will be encountered in one form or another according to the needs and nature of the initiate.

Amongst the philosophers who accorded credence to the Egyptian mysteries, Philo, Plutarch and Plato probably feature the most. Philo, a Jewish Hellenistic scholar, was an apologist for the Therapeuts, a healing branch of the Essenes (30-20 B.C.), and it is to him that we owe much of the information available today concerning the occult activities of that order. His comments include the concepts of an active and a passive causation principle at the god source, the logos being the son of this father/mother god responsible for our solar system and all movements therein, via the physical Sun.

Plutarch the Greek, who lived in the second half of the first century A.D., chose Isis and Osiris as his subject. He was an occultist priest of the order of Apollo and Dionysus, and thus well versed in the magical procedures of both systems and their attendant mysteries.

In one very informative and fruitful essay, written at Delphi and addressed to a priestess by the name of Klea, he proved most enlightening. Klea, it would appear, held a distinguished position among the Delphic priestesses and had also been initiated into the Osiriac mysteries. It has been speculated that Plutarch probably based much of his occult information on one of Manetho's treatises on the old Egyptian religion because, like Manetho, he writes as a commentator rather than a dogmatist, covering many different aspects and interpretations of the mythology and symbology. A few interesting magical details emerged from this particular essay; for example, it was established that Klea's robes were white, ornamented with blue and gold, and that members of the priesthood did not wear wool but had their robes made from flax, a vegetable. Neither did they eat meat. Diluted wine was drunk in this order, but only very seldom and never before magical or religious work. Water was considered impure on account of the living organisms within it that caused pollution, something the priests seemed fully aware of even in those distant times. Lesser ranks ate fish, it appears, but not the high priests. It is always interesting to know the magical disciplines and procedures employed in such times, especially when considering suitable modes for the expression of these same occult principles in our present day and age.

It is to Plutarch that we owe most of the Isis/Osiris information which had obviously been culled from former fragments now extinct. The story of the famous game of draughts played prior to the birth of the gods, for example, with its resulting intercalary days. Plutarch even informs his readers as to which gods were born on which days. Osiris was first, Horus second (according to this legend Horus was conceived in love by Isis and Osiris while they themselves were still in the womb), Set was third, Isis fourth and Nephthys fifth. Earlier sources tend to include Thoth in place of Horus, thus supporting the later story of Horus's birth after the dethronement of Osiris by Set.

Plutarch continues to give all the versions he had obviously read, with the idea, no doubt, of allowing the reader to draw his or her own conclusions as to which one, if any, was accurate. One interesting mention worthy of occult investigation is Horus's choice of animal to accompany him on his quest for the destruction of his father's enemy, Set. Osiris is reported to have enquired of his son as to which animal he would prefer and Horus to have replied 'a white horse'. Somewhat nonplussed by this answer, Osiris requested an explanation as to why his own animal symbol, the lion, was not preferred. Horus told his father: 'Lion is a needful thing to one requiring help, but horse (can) scatter in pieces the foe in flight and consume him utterly,' which answer appeared to please Osiris greatly. Osiris is also reputed to have put the question to his son as to what he considered was a just and fair task in life and the answer to have been 'helping father and mother in ill plight', which was again the right thing to say. Occultly speaking, the horse represents purified passion and the lion receptive power of the mind; therein lies a deeply significant magical truth for those whose minds are capable of penetrating its hidden meaning.

The Trismegistus teaching accords specific colouring to each of the gods. Set is always mentioned as having reddish skin and red hair; Osiris a tanned complexion but fairish hair; Isis dark-haired but fair-skinned and blue-eyed; Nephthys fairish and green-eyed; and Horus very fair and blue-eyed after the nature of Apollo, Baldur and all the Sun gods.

Fixed stars and constellations receive mention in relation to the respective influences of the gods: Sirius for Isis; Orion for Horus and the Bear for Set. These have the ring of later appellations, Apollo being a skilled archer and corresponding to Horus, according to the Greeks etc., so it might not be advisable to pay too much attention to them.

Plutarch deals with both the Orphic rites and the Eleusinia and his correspondences are interesting. Osiris he equates with Pluto or Dionysus (the Greeks seemed to favour this association generally), while he sees Demeter in the Orphic role, probably because they both went the same way about reclaiming a lost love from the underworld.

That the flood was caused by the machinations of Set seems to have been generally regarded as true by most of the early commentators on things Egyptian. If one could look at the Osiris myth as relating to the inundation of light (Atlantis or wherever) by darkness (Set), causing a withdrawal of the force of light to a higher region until such times as it can be restored by a renewed bout of solar energy (Horus), signifying a change in the axial rotation of the Earth that might cause the sunken land to rise again and give up its secrets, one might get a clearer picture of how the early Egyptians, or their teachers, endeavoured to convey cosmic or cosmological truths in parable form.

Plutarch also mentions the sistrum, a magical instrument of great importance in the Egyptian system and one which I shall be covering in detail in a later chapter. Speaking of the symbolism of the sistrum he says: 'The sistrum also shows that existent things must be shaken up and never have cessation from impulse, but as it were be awakened up and agitated when they fall asleep and die away. For they say they turn aside and beat off Typhon (Set) with sistra, signifying that when corruption binds nature fast and brings her to a stand, (then) generation frees her and raises her from death by means of motion.

'Now the sistrum has a curved top, and its arch contains the four (things) that are shaken. For the part of the cosmos which is subject to generation and corruption, is circumscribed by the sphere of the moon, and all (things) in it are moved and changed by the four elements – fire and earth and water and air. (The link between the sistrum and the occult law of abundance is made quite clear here.) And on the arch of the sistrum, at the top, they put the metal figure of a cat with a human face, and at the bottom, below the shaken things, the face sometimes of Isis and sometimes of Nephthys, symbolizing by the faces generation and consummation (for these are the changes and motions of the elements), and by the cat the moon, on account of the variable nature, night habits and fecundity of the beast.'

After further observations concerning the nocturnal habits of felines Plutarch ends his little piece about the sistrum with 'and by the human face of the cat is signified the intellectual and reasonable nature of the changes that take place in connection with the moon.'

Some of all this is quite feasible in the light of present day knowledge, but one has to sort the wheat from the chaff. There is no doubt, however, that we owe much to Plutarch for, in his capacity as professional journalist of the period, he has certainly reported all he heard without fear or favour and, as is ever the case, the student is left to select the inner meanings and dispense with the outer layers or colourings of the historical period during which the reporting was done.

The last volume in Book 1 is entitled *The Shepherd of Hermas*. Purportedly an ancient Egyptian script, it circulated among the Gnostics and Essenes who espoused many of its teachings. It tends to be rather too philosophically obscure to be of any real use to the student of magic and, apart from the Aeon doctrine which presents some interesting ideas on evolution, it inclines to metaphysical meanderings of the sort that are all rather too suspiciously unfounded in logic.

Plato also acknowledged the wisdom of Hermes, especially in relation to the doctrine of reincarnation. Hermes, Plato tells us, taught that man needed several lives or incarnations in which to learn the necessary lessons and, although he does mention other Hermetic teachings, it was mainly that of rebirth that caught his attention and evoked his sagacious comments.

Book 2 of *The Hermes Trismegistus* is entitled the *Corpus Hermeticum* or body of the literature. Its first works appear as a set of sermons and letters that have been translated and pre-served by one called Poemandres. Nobody rightly knows who this person was, or even if a single person answering to this nomenclature ever existed, because in Egyptian the name means 'a witness'. Poemandres, it is explained, underwent a psychic experience when Hermes instructed him to bring the ancient texts up to date, and the first instalment is entitled *The Shepherd of Men*.

The god-mind, Poemandres tells us, is male and female, the female aspect being the Sophia or wisdom and the male the Christos or will. It would seem that this gentleman was as con-vinced about the divine source of his revelations as Christians are about the holy spirit hovering perfunctorily over them when they translate or endeavour to interpret the scriptures.

He has quite a bit to say about the evolution of intelligent life on this planet. The first men, he states, were etheric and their bodies were composed of fire and air. They were also hermaphroditical.The beasts or animals evolved at one end of the scale and these etheric people at the other. The animals slowly ascended the evolutionary ladder while the etheric folk 'descended' until the two met and one was able to ensoul the body of the other, thus endowing it with a high intelligence or different type or grade of psyche or soul.

This document dates the 'shepherd' archetype as decidedly pre-Christian and also ties in Hermes with the biblical Melchisadek. It is worth perusal, if only to note its similarities to later ideologies. Of course it could be argued that, as the authenticity of much of this literature is often questioned in relation to the times in which it was purportedly written, any conjectures are purely academic and, therefore, only the essence or hidden meaning should be sought for and extracted.

Our next incursion into the Trismegistic literature introduces us to Stobaeus, his first contribution taking the form of a dialogue between Hermes and Asclepius in which the master instructs the pupil in the mysteries of the cosmos and the spiritual development and progression of the soul. This section contains some information that is certainly worthy of note, especially to the aspiring occultist. The Egyptian priesthood was not a celibate one, the general belief being that a man should discharge his duty to society and live a practical, political and social life to the full before retiring to contemplation. Begetting children was a good idea, it seems, especially among old or advanced souls who were more likely to bring evolved spirits into incarnation, or ensure that children born to them were raised in the correct spiritual perspective. It was generally felt that advanced souls could better express their wisdom if born into spiritually favourable circumstances. The Hermetic teachings generally are against celibacy in any form, as they strictly advocate the law of polarity in both the spiritual and secular context.

Here again we have the constantly repeating theme of the flood, the master race that dwelt before it occurred, and a knowledge of astronomy comparable to a standard only attainable with the aid of an advanced technology.

Titillating pieces of information in the *Corpus Hermeticum* include references to the first concept or 'god' as a solar deity with stellar features; the imperishable nature of the psyche or spirit; the etheric body; reincarnation and why; animals and people being of separate evolutionary streams and *not* inter-mingling; overcoming karma by will; energy and matter; the race of logos or devas and – probably the most interesting of all – the dual nature of the soul. Hermes tells us that only one fragment of our spirit actually enters the earthly time circuits, while the other part remains in a state of timelessness. Modern esoteric teachings concerning higher selves, and all that, possibly stem from this kind of doctrine, but care should be taken not to confuse one's own 'higher self' with the many other intelligences in the universe, or life tends to become one big ego trip.

By far the most interesting of all three Trismegistic books is volume 3 which includes *The Virgin of the World, The Sermon of Isis to Horus,* and various fragments from early scholars and commentators.

Many believers in the Egyptian system, your author included, are of the opinion that much of this information is prophetic and does not relate to past occurrences, either pre-Egyptian or cosmological. The philosophy and magical concepts are very advanced and more suited to generations ahead of the present day than to the apparently primitive cultures of the past. Let us take some examples:

1. The complete equality of the sexes, the teaching being that the spirit may select a body of either sex according to its evolutionary needs.

2. References to certain branches of the animal kingdoms being of a higher evolutionary grade than others, notably lions and dolphins.

3. Man's pollution of the planet which results in a revolt by the four elements.

4. The 'old ones' whose origins were not of this world and from whom, according to his mother Isis, Horus and his divine family sprang.

5. How wise spirits were originally ordained to occupy places of power and responsibility, but their power was usurped by younger and less experienced souls who gained their position by the use of force (the Osiris/Set situation acted out amongst mankind?).

6. Of the nature of males and females, the elements predominant in each of the sexes and how these should rightly manifest according to cosmic law.

7. The chakras of the planet Earth.
8. Our planet as a body, subject to imbalances and diseases but also curable.
9. Connecting illness with the four elements and healing with the balancing of these within man.
10. The etheric world preceding the physical one: as above so below.
11. The 'gods' who descended from 'heaven' to teach mankind via Hermes and then returned to their original home.
12. Books translated from some 'sacred language' into the then modern tongue (prior to the first dynasty).
13. The word 'Khem' (Egypt) meaning 'blackland' or land of dark people, and 'Khemu', land of Mu where there are dark people; it is also the root of the word 'chemistry': black art.
14. Evidence that the mathematical nature of the universe was well understood.
15. The wheel of karma.
16. The folly of intellectual nit-picking.
17. The nature of cosmic law.
18. The zodiac.
19. The family of devic spirits of archangels from another solar system.
20. The nature of disease.

These are but a few of the exciting and magically stimulating teachings to be found in this extraordinary work. It would seem logical to suppose that in accordance with normal Egyptian magical procedures the instructress (Isis) assumes the role of the goddess in addressing her son, Horus (the student), so we are not necessarily dealing with trance lectures or spook-inspired doctrines but with the verbal (and latterly recorded) features of a sound and very old magical tradition.

The final references in *The Hermes Trismegistus*, Volume 3, also contain some interesting themes. *Justin Martyr* (A.D. 100-165) refers to the 'gods' as 'sons of god' and states that Isis, Osiris, Hermes and their family were 'sons of god' who had a specific role to play in the universal evolutionary scheme and a separate task in relation to man.

Clement of Alexandria (A.D. 150-220) tells us that the gods

Hermes, Ptah and Imhotep once lived amongst men in Egypt to which they came from a land before the flood. Hermes, the learned father informs us, brought from those lands certain books of a medical nature that were absolutely indispensable. These were forty-two in number. Six-and-thirty of them, containing the whole wisdom discipline of the Egyptians, are learned by heart by the (grades of priests) already mentioned. The remaining six are learned by the shrine-bearers (physicians); these are the medical treatises dealing with:

37. The constitution of the body.
38. Diseases.
39. Instruments.
40. Drugs.
41. Eyes.
42. The maladies of women.

Tertullian (A.D. 160-230) states that Hermes taught Plato and that the doctrine of reincarnation dated back to a civilization that existed before the flood.

Cyprian (A.D. 200-258) tells us that 'thrice greatest Hermes' understood the nature of the one God which, he felt, was normally beyond human understanding.

Lactantius (fourth century A.D.) speaks of Hermes, saying that the month of September was sacred to him and that he ruled the sign of Virgo jointly with Isis. References are also made in this fragment to the elemental and deva kingdoms and to two kinds of good and evil.

Cyril of Alexandria (A.D. 412-444) backs up the Christian father, Cyprian, regarding Hermes being called 'thrice great' because he understood the true nature of the trinity.

So much for the Christian fathers. The philosophers were also generous in their mention of this Egyptian teaching.

Zosimus (third/fourth century A.D.) refers to Hermes as being of the kingdom of devas or archangels, a being who taught man all matters medical far in advance of primitive understanding. Reference is also made here to a 'counterfeit daimon' who leads men astray but whom Hermes knew how to combat.

Iamblichus (A.D. 255-330). We shall deal with him in a separate chapter.

Julian, the emperor (reigned A.D. 360-363), claims that

Hermes was a 'guide' from the higher planes of spirit and not a person or early king. He also states that Hermes may teach at any age in the history of man through the inspiration of a medium. This emperor saw the 'sons of god' as archangels or devas rather than beings from outer space, but this is logical when one considers the current trends of religion and philosophy that prevailed during his reign, and the strength of character he must have needed to hold out against the oncoming tide of Christianity.

From the aforegoing it must be obvious to the student of all things Egyptian that a wealth of knowledge lies hidden within the Trismegistic teachings, knowledge that is invaluable to the true seeker into the Egyptian magical arts. Egyptian magic is essentially cosmic and not tribal or parochial and, in order to comprehend magical concepts that reach out beyond this world, it is necessary to conceive of other worlds beyond our own and their place in the universal scheme of things. The magi of old obviously knew all about this, but kept their wisdom for select pupils until the 'time' was right. But, again, this information has always been there. Perhaps it has been protected from prying eyes by the 'shield of invisibility', the mantle of Nephthys in the Egyptian system or the helmet of invisibility in the Greek system.

It has been postulated that no knowledge is ever lost. Forgotten, maybe, to be relearned at some time appropriate to its replacement in and relevancy to the history and evolution of this planet. Someone remarked to me recently that occultists or magicians and the like were superfluous because 'divine plans' were carried through regardless of the machinations of men. That's as maybe, but then these so-termed 'divine plans' are usually conceived by the 'gods' and carried out on their behalf through the offices of less exalted souls, often at their own peril. But, if all time is one time, justice and injustice are in continual balance. It is only because of our individual isolation in one pocket of time that we appear to experience an overdose of one side of the scale.

10. THE EGYPTIAN MYSTERIES ACCORDING TO IAMBLICHOS

This superlative work by Iamblichos was translated from the Greek by Alexander Wilder, M.D., F.A.S., and first published in 1911. It consists of a series of dialogues between Porphyry, distinguished scholar and foremost writer in the later Platonic school, and one Anebo.

Porphyry, *circa* A.D. 232-304, was a native of Tyre and his name Molech, or king, was rendered by Longinus into 'Porphurios', denoting the royal purple, as a proper equivalent. He was a disciple of Plotinus who later broadened his philosophic interests to include other beliefs. In his personal life he followed the Pythagorean discipline. He was a severe critic of the Gnostic beliefs then current, including with them the newly popularized Christian faith. Being essentially a mystic, he regarded the ceremonial rites of the Egyptian theurgy with mistrust. He favoured Mithraism, while Iamblichos followed the cult of Serapis which was then the state religion in Egypt.

The scribe himself, Iamblichos, is said to have lived around A.D. 255-330 but the exact dates are not known and therefore, strictly speaking, this period is conjectural.

Of Anebo we know little. He is referred to as an Egyptian priest and his name is that of Anubis, psychopompos and guardian of the sacred literature. Porphyry addressed him as 'prophet' or servant of divinity and expounder of the sacred oracles; it is in this capacity that the philosopher sought his explanations regarding the Egyptian theosophical doctrines, religious beliefs and magical rites.

This enlightening and fascinating dialogue commences with the words of Porphyry: 'I will begin this friendly correspondence with thee with a view to learning what is believed in respect to the gods and good daemons and likewise the various philosophic speculations in regard to them. Many things have been set forth concerning these subjects by the (Grecian) philosophers, but they for the most part have derived the substance of their belief from conjecture.' The learned man then proceeded to list his queries which, as one might imagine, contained a goodly share of Greek logic and, in essence, questioned the knowledge and efficacy of a system that was magically based and orientated.

In reply to Porphyry's letter to Anebo, one Abammon, the teacher, was obviously charged with the apology and opens his answering epistle with the following words: 'Hermes, the patron of literature, was rightly considered of old to be a god common to all the priests and the one presiding over the genuine learning relating to the gods, one and the same among all. Hence our predecessors were wont to ascribe to him their discoveries in wisdom and to name all their respective works *Books of Hermes*.'

The 'priests' referred to in these dialogues consisted of many orders, including the performers of rites (magi), prophets, the learned professions, philosophers, poets, authors, physicians, master mechanics etc. In fact, the Egyptian priesthood embraced far more than just the occult, and the necessity for this balance was well realized from early times.

It would be impossible to cover even a section of this document and do it justice, but I feel it to be of some importance that the essence of the deeper Egyptian beliefs are highlighted, as they form a sound basis for the practice of the accompanying rites and certainly help the student to find his or her way around the meaningful rituals we shall be looking at later.

Despite the antiquity of the Egyptian teaching it is neither patriarchal nor matriarchal but equally balanced, which opens the door to aspirants of either sex. Great emphasis is placed upon an understanding of the many forms of evolution likely to be encountered while on magical excursions. In other words, it is not all man's world, meaning *Homo sapiens*. There are numerous classes of spirits and some of the names given to them by this Egyptian priest have been borrowed from the Greeks.

This is not surprising considering the cultural interchanges of the period but, as the message is roughly the same as in the earliest Recension of *The Book of the Dead*, the semantics are irrelevant.

We are treated, in the first place, to a description of the gods, devas, spirits of the elements, heroes, and a host of other invisible forces that go to bridge the gap between mankind and the universe beyond him. Many of these intelligencies, or energies, govern from without and do not themselves enter human bodies. Neither does the human body contain the soul but the other way around, the body being actually contained by the spirit, which immediately suggests a relationship between the spirit and the force fields surrounding the physical body that are now recognizable with the aid of modern technological equipment.

It has ever been the habit of man to compartmentalize and, in theological application, this no doubt helps many people to create their gods in their own image and likeness instead of the other way round. Paul, in his epistle to the Ephesians, does a neat little pigeon-holing job and his list runs as follows: 1. Princes. 2. Authorities. 3. Kosmocrators or princes of the cosmos. 4. Spiritual essences in the super celestial spheres.

Christians later classified their angelic kingdoms into nine choirs, but the Egyptian priests were on to this one centuries earlier. We are told by Scutellius that there were nine classes of spiritual beings according to the ancient tradition: 1. Invisible gods. 2. Visible gods of the sky (planets?). 3. Archangels. 4. Angels. 5. Demons. 6. Leaders. 7. Princes. 8. Heroes or demigods. 9. Souls.

Masmakios enumerates six orders of the Chaldean categories as follows: 1. Gods that are pure mind. 2. The gods subsisting before all subordinate dominion. 3. Rulers. 4. Archangels. 5. Divinities that are confined to no specific place or service. 6. Divinities or geniuses with specific duties.

The ancient Sadducees also believed in angel emanations and many aspects of one divinity, as their deity was invoked in the required aspect rather than as a saint or individualized patron, a theory to which Plato also subscribed.

There are lots more groups of classifications which date back to these early periods and before, which, of course, the medieval occultists had a hey-day with later on, much to the chagrin of the genuine student of Egyptian magic. The point to be made is obviously that, from the earliest time, the mystery teachings have considered the universe to be an orderly place in which an infinite number of life forms, intelligences existing outside the confines of matter, and evolutionary permutations co-exist and are interdependent one upon another.

At all junctures in the study of Egyptian philosophy and magic one encounters the importance of the spirits of the elements – air, fire, earth and water – and their place in the magical scheme of things. It was also considered necessary to be able to know and recognize the forces of evil, or the principle of evil, in order to combat it, a doctrine not at all in keeping with some pseudo-social and highly questionable 'mystic' cults of today.

Astrology deserves a chapter to itself, but suffice it to say that the Egyptians had their own answers, these being more of a philosophic than predictive nature. Nor were any of the planets considered to be 'malignant' in the generally accepted astrological meaning of the word, one example given being that a man suffering from scurvy who sits in the heat of the Sun will increase his sufferings, but it is not the Sun that causes the additional discomfort, it is the scurvy in the man. Thus with, say, Saturn the teacher, if we feel put out by his influences, it is because we, like the slack pupil, have not learned our lessons from him and need to be brought into line rather firmly. It is also the nature of all things that are partial or incomplete (in the process of evolution and not yet fully attained to the ultimate or godhead) to decompose and undergo change. Therefore, the spirits, essences or energies governing those changes are not agents of evil but simply servants of natural law, each doing its duty without fear or favour.

Our one connecting link with the gods and with the universe as a whole is, we are told, *mind*. There exists within each individual the potential to reach forth and link with the universal consciousness and, through channels thus opened, to draw upon the forces of life contained therein, either for self-healing or in service to others. Of course such energies can be drawn and 'misplaced', which in our language means they have been used against cosmic law or for 'evil' purposes. But the forces themselves are neither evil nor good. They are simply forces or energies. Only the intention behind their manipulation colours them.

When it came to the question of invoking the aid of discarnate entities or beings from other spheres or levels within the universe, the Egyptians did not approve of this practice being carried out *ad lib* without the necessary know-how regarding what one was calling forth or how to control it, assuming that it arrived on time. In the *Timaeus* Plato declares that the faculty of divining is active only when the understanding or reasoning faculty is in abeyance, fettered by sleep or alienated by disease or the entheastic rapture. Plutarch imputes its activity to a certain crisis or condition of body through which it becomes separated from the consciousness of objects and matters that are immediately present. This is extremely interesting when viewed in the light of modern scientific knowledge of the human brain and its functions. The left hemisphere is, we are told, associated with the reasoning and logical thinking factors such as mathematics, all practical concerns and our day-to-day routine, while the right hemisphere governs the more abstract and creative side of the human psyche.

Just as the left hemisphere would appear to respond primarily to inner time (clock time etc.) so the right hemisphere is programmed to function in outer time or cosmic timelessness. Recent experiments with patients who have had the two hemispheres surgically separated show that each side of the brain can function independently of the other, and that the right hemisphere is capable of producing answers to questions before they have been put to it. Taking this into consideration, in the light of the knowledge and observations of the Egyptian priests, we come up with a pretty sound basis for believing their knowledge to have originated with a people possessing a very high standard of technology in addition to a sophisticated philosophy and accompanying magical *cultus*.

Anebo goes quite deeply into the question of so-called 'trance' revelations, taking into account the levels at which the medium is likely to contact or establish a link with the 'gods' or lesser spirits floating about the cosmos. The ancient Egyptians didn't make too much of a habit of including this type of mediumship in their magical practices and were, it would seem, particularly fussy as to whom they allowed to be used as 'channels' for the gods. They also realized that there are just as many imposters in other dimensions as we are likely to encounter in our daily earthly lives. Intelligences from the higher spheres are not given to producing phenomena; and mirrors, crystals and other such psychic aids are a constant source of error and deception according to the ancient Egyptian priests; emblems, however, are safe, as they are often used as vehicles of divine power.

Perhaps it might benefit those who complain that they do not get the answers they wish for from psychic sources to take note of the comments made by Anebo when he was questioned regarding the oft-times unco-operative nature of the oracles. It is sometimes necessary for us to live our lives for ourselves and not lean too heavily on other minds who, after all, have their own thing to do. If the gods in their wisdom see fit to deny us access to outer time, then it is usually because of some decision made by our own free will or spirit, maybe even prior to entering the body.

A clear line of demarcation is made between what the Egyptian priest refers to as 'other parts of the soul' i.e., the 'higher self', and those who guide or watch over us. Too many people appear only too happy to ascribe all forms of inspiration to some exalted aspect of themselves, so care should be taken to locate the difference and carefully observe it.

The type of psychic phenomenon that obviously made its presence felt at the sacred rites of the period is well described in this work. Any experienced occultist will have worked with the four elements, probably finding greater affinity with one in particular, and it would appear that in those far gone times the principle was exactly the same. The temple magi obviously made a better job of teaching their pupils how to recognize what they were likely to come up against than many present day lodges. Having picked up the pieces resulting from dabblers' misfortunes on more than one occasion, I cannot help feeling that the old temple ways were the correct ones; or should be until such times as man can exert a degree of self-discipline in an occult situation.

Porphyry didn't go much on phenomena of any kind and questioned Anebo as to why all that sort of stuff was necessary. Surely, he postulates, the gods, if they are what they are claimed to be, do not need to disturb water in bowls, project bizarre images into magic mirrors or appear as insubstantial phantasms calculated to scare the daylights out of the average person. A valid point, indeed, and who wants all that junk anyway? True communication with the higher spheres is always mind to mind, and when the table starts rapping one can usually cast a pretty good guess as to the level of the communicator. Of course, the old Egyptian magicians knew that all the 'bumps in the night' stuff was not the real thing and took the appropriate precautions against it. Any occultist worthy of his or her salt knows how to inhibit phenomena or, in other words, block out the slower frequencies.

In addition to their feelings about divination, the Egyptians also had strong views regarding states of ecstasy induced by devotional approaches to the rites. While the necessity for some to imbibe the atmosphere of overt devotionalism was accepted, any accompanying outward display or resulting abreaction was considered purely in the therapeutic context and not truly relevant to magic proper in its 'controlled' form.

Freewill and how it operates is commented upon, as Plato said in *Republic:* 'The choice of the earthly condition is made by the soul itself, and very generally it differs from what it has been in the preceding term of life in this world. The cause is in him who makes the choice and *the divinity is without blame in the matter*. After the choice has been made, the "daimon" or guardian angel is allotted.'

The tendency for us mortals to judge beings from the higher realms by emotion is faulty, we are told. Earthly emotions do not necessarily bear any relationship to cosmic laws or the way things are outside our own time zone.

Anebo had a lot to say about healing power and considered the gift to belong to the individual and not to powers transmitted via the medium from some guide or discarnate entity. The priests of ancient Egypt, it would appear, used dream therapy and hypnosis to effect their cures and in some of the temples of the god Asculapius he was renamed Oneiropompos, the sender of dreams. At these centres of healing there were 'sleep houses' where incubation therapy was employed in much the same way as it is used in modern Swiss clinics. Care should be taken, however, when analysing dreams, to distinguish between the tension releasing mechanisms of the subconscious mind and genuine time travelling.

Egyptian priests understood the principles of levitation quite well and, according to reports from his disciples, Iamblichos himself was able to levitate several feet when he prayed. Not that this was considered as essential for magical practices; on the contrary, the Hermetic teaching rather scorned occult show-offs.

Music at the arcane rites also received mention, indicating a deeper knowledge of the effect of certain rhythms and sounds on the chakras. Frenzied reactions do *not* make for good magic which essentially calls for a cool head and clear control of both hemispheres of the brain. Certain ecstatic cults, notably the Korybantes, employed music of a stimulating nature guaranteed to over-emphasize the functions of the *muladhara* chakra; but not the genuine Egyptian rites, which favoured quieter and gentler sounds. Only the tinkle of the sistrum was likely to disturb the tranquillity of an Egyptian temple working, and that is good magic. The stirring up of uncontrollable passions is guaranteed to attract energies or intelligences of an equally uncontrollable nature (like attracts like), which gets one absolutely nowhere. But then, I suppose, it all depends where one wants to get to, or what one wants to do with any forces that might respond to one's invocation or evocation. If one is working on the path of light the answer must be 'use it or them for the fullest possible benefit of all things and in the unsullied cause of light and love'. That might be *my* motto, but how each and every person who chooses to practise magic decides to colour his or her intentions will be between them and Thoth, lord of karma.

The Hermeticists were in agreement with the Platonic school regarding sacrifice, and were totally against blood offerings. Therefore any blood sacrificial references carry the hallmark of pagan or primitive infusions. The Egyptians conceived of the idea of the animal soul being able to ascend the evolutionary ladder within its own kind, on other planets if not on Earth, so therefore they were well able to accept animal spirit communicators without logical rejection. Strangely enough, according to Anebo, the Egyptian temple workers carried out a form of 'rescue work' rather like that employed by spiritualists today. The priests worked by 'fetching' the right spiritual helpers who then took over.

The lotus as a symbol is not limited to the East, as is commonly thought. The Egyptians used it centuries ago and often depicted a person seated upon a lotus, signifying mind over matter. The lotus was the symbol of mind. The winged disk was a solar symbol. Certain symbols were said to contain occult secrets made known only to the higher priests. One such 'mystery' concerned the helio-centric theory and the connecting link between our own Sun and the sun or star of another system.

There was a sacred language used by the priests which was said to be the remnants of an archaic tongue long since forgotten. Some of this later crept into the Eleusinia, the term *konx om pax*, for example, that has perplexed scholars for years but is generally known to students of Egyptian magic as an expression of supreme truth that can be traced to the old Akkad root language.

Later Egyptian priests, notably Anebo and his contemporaries, did not follow the same deities as, say, the Middle Kingdom period, when Amon and Mut reigned supreme at Thebes. The much older Memphis triad found favour again, with Bast assuming the role of consort to Ptah and Imhotep then firmly established as their healer-son.

The wisdom of Anebo will be obvious to anyone who takes the trouble to seek out and read this enlightening work. He deals with the nature of evil, karma brought over from former lives and – much to the disappointment of many – the fact that the 'path' is *not* for everyone. Iamblichos himself, in his *Life of Pythagoras*, remarks that 'he who pours clean water into a muddy well does but disturb the mud', thus very much agreeing with Jesus's charge to his disciples not to give the holy truth to dogs, nor cast pearls before swine, 'for the latter will tread the jewels under their feet and the dogs will rend the uncautious givers'. Oh dear, not a doctrine that will be at all well received in this age of equality, or endeavoured equality perhaps I should say. Unfortunately for the hard working equalizers the cosmos is *not* equal at any given point in time. This does not mean that we don't all end up at a similar stage at some point or other during our evolutionary cycle. But from the magical point of view all people are not at an identical stage in their spiritual development. Some are better suited to pursue the path while others are either not ready for it, undergoing a life of rest from it, or simply here to do other things this time round. After all, we can't all be ballet dancers, composers, architects or doctors. It takes all sorts to make a world and over many lifetimes we play many roles. However, some schools of magic do subscribe to the idea of the unchanging nature of the soul so that if one is basically of, say, a priestly caste, although one may enjoy many lives outside the temple walls one's basic attitudes will always contain a grain of religion of one kind or another. Equally, if one is by nature of spirit a sage, then that sagacity will out either in a local amateur dramatic society, as factory bench philosopher or village wise-woman. It does not always have to be expressed in the positive mode.

Mr Wilder's unquestionable erudition renders the notes and comments in this work worthy of a study in themselves and, for those of scholarly leanings who like to tie in correspondences between the Egyptian system and philosophies and rites of other concurrent beliefs, a detailed study of these is thoroughly recommended.

The Egyptian Mysteries, by Iamblichos, is truly an enlightening and profound work, and a study of its deeper meaning is recommended to all who would tread the magical path in the Egyptian robes.

PART TWO
THE PRACTICE

11. SYMBOLS AND INSTRUMENTS

There are certain magical emblems that belong almost exclusively to the Egyptian system. Some of these have crept into popular decorative art of late mainly because of exposure at international exhibitions, scientific interest in ancient theories, and a tendency among the young to look back to old beliefs for inspiration. The impedimenta required by the practitioner of the Egyptian occult arts need not be complex, however, even in the pursuit of ritual magic, and not all Egyptian magic is ritually based as we shall see.

The following items and symbols are the most commonly used and constitute a good basis for Egyptian magical practices:

The Sistrum

The sistrum (*plural* sistra) is an instrument shaped like an ankh with four bars suspended across the loop head (later representations often appear with only three but these are incorrect). These bars fit loosely in their sockets so that when the instrument is shaken, using the lower part as a handle, the four loose bars act as a sort of rattle. Small bells or cymbals are often strung across the bars in tambourine-style. The dictionary describes the sistrum as 'a jingling instrument of thin metal frame with transverse loose metal rods and a handle by which it is shaken, used especially in Egypt in the worship of Isis'. Plutarch's description of the sistrum we have already examined and according to early historians its origin was unknown. Its message, however, did seep through and it was considered to be emblematic of the principles that not only generate the universe but keep it in equipoise. These principles are called the male and female in nature, the positive and negative in science, and the active and passive in metaphysics. Their blending produced a universal harmony heard only by the gods and called, according to the Platonic theory, 'the music of the spheres'.

The sistrum has connections with three goddesses: Isis, Hathor and Bast. But, as it is more often than not depicted with the figure of a cat, its closest association is with the cat goddess. One legend has it that it was a gift to Bast from her divine mother, Isis, its allocation to Hathor only occurring in much later times.

According to psychic sources the four bars on the sistrum were originally tuned to four musical notes that corresponded with the four elements, and these were struck and not shaken. At some point in the Atlantean past it must have had sonic connections, more likely directed towards altering states of human consciousness than affecting the structure of material objects. In Egyptian magic the sistrum is the sacred instrument of the magician who has mastered the element of fire and who works primarily through the Bast ray via this element. If used in the Isis or Hathor context the element changes, but this again would be governed by the natural occult 'calling' of the user. For example, an occultist wishing to employ a Hathor ritual, who is by nature more in harmony with the element of air, should *not* use the sistrum to invoke the element of fire. As a principle magical instrument, I can but repeat, it is best employed in the fiery context in conjunction with the Bast ray.

A good average size for the sistrum is around twelve inches from top to bottom, but the loop must be in exact proportion to the handle. It can be made of wood, brass, silver or any alloy. In Egypt sistra were originally silver or gold. I have a brass ceremonial sistrum surmounted by a cat figure and a secular wooden one mounted in a pyramid-shaped base. One of these was constructed by a professional musical instrument maker and the other by a maker of occult impedimenta. Anyone possessing the necessary skills can make their own and there are several specimens available for viewing in the British Museum.

The Winged Disk

Emblematic of the element of air, this consists of a circle or solar-type disk enclosed by a pair of wings. In ritual magic it is suspended over the altar in an easterly direction and used when invoking the protection and co-operation of the sylphs. It can come in any workable size, and the wings should be silver in colour with a yellow central disk.

The Cup or Chalice

In all magical workings the cup or chalice represents the element of water. It is also the tool of the 'scryer' in the Egyptian system and should be handled by the celebrant and scryer only. It is best made of a silver-colour metal and should always contain pure, clear water when in ritual use.

The Mirror of Hathor

A variation of the shield, this is a highly powerful and significant piece of magical equipment. Ideally, it should be made of solid bronze, with the face of the goddess at the top of the handle supporting the mirror itself, which appears in the solar disk form. One side of the mirror is polished and reflective; the other side is slightly scoured. It has several uses in Egyptian magic: reflecting back unwanted thoughts or energies to the sender, protecting against enemies and summoning the element of earth, or gnome kingdom, are the main ones. In size it should be roughly the same as the sistrum but a good deal heavier, of course. There is a superb example of a Hathor mirror in the British Museum for those who would like to view one. When the altar is laid for ceremonial magic each instrument should be placed according to its elemental correspondence and point of the compass.

The Wand

Although the sistrum is associated with the fire element it is not necessarily the sacred instrument with which the salamanders are summoned. There should always be an open flame of some kind, but only if the celebrant is akin to fire should the sistrum be used as a wand. If he or she is closer to the nature of water the crook or flail becomes the wand; if airy, the caduceus; and, if earthy, the djed or ankh. So it is essential that the aspiring magician knows a little, at least, about himself and has ascertained his basic cosmic elemental roots.

The Uraeus

This symbol is said to represent a stage of achieved awareness or inner sight and an ability to command the universe. It should only be worn by the initiated soul who has attained to a certain degree of universal wisdom and understanding. It is another version of the eye of Horus, or sacred eye of Ra. Some scholars consider the uraeus to be the right eye and the Horus eye the left. My advice is to leave it alone if you are not sure. If you know your way around the cosmos, then employ the uraeus in your ceremony. One other thing: the stones in the eyes of the serpent should vary in colour with the nature of the wearer. Which colour for whom, you may ask? That I cannot tell you. It is usually revealed at a certain stage in Egyptian initiation but, if you use a ruby eye when you should have used a clear crystal, you could be in for magical complications from the elements of fire and water.

The Crook and Flail

These are the traditional symbols of Osiris and they have several meanings. In addition to the temporal powers normally awarded to them they are fertility emblems associated with the planting of seeds and resulting harvest and, as Osiris was a water divinity, their moistening quality is obvious. Both crook and flail should be approximately the same length and in balance with each other. The crook should be coloured predominantly in solar tints, or gilt, and the flail in silver and blue, the latter of either a lapis or turquoise hue. There are plenty of pictures in popular Egyptian art books that show the crook and flail quite clearly and the aspiring magician can make up his or her own according to personal inclination as regards size, design etc. The most important thing is to keep the colour scheme correct.

The Eye of Horus

Often referred to as the utchat (or udjat), eyes have always been sacred in Egyptian teachings. The first eye to receive mention in the old Egyptian fable is that of Ra, the Creator, so it would seem that this is a cosmological symbol and not strictly belonging to the planet Earth. It has strong healing connotations and should always be employed in any therapeutic ceremony or practice. The name 'utchat' is said by one reference to mean 'to be in good mental and physical health'. Utchats were buried with the mummies in olden times, as it was believed that they ensured strength and vitality to the spirit during its journeys through the realms of darkness to the kingdom of Osiris. One legend has it that it was bestowed on Horus by Ra and that Horus, in turn, allowed his twin sister, Bast, to wear it for him, thus conferring on her the gift of healing. Horus was also a healer god, but his powers were more of a physical nature whereas Bast was essentially a healer of the mind. The beneficial effect of the kindred of Bast (the cat family) upon the mentally ill has been observed by physicians down the ages. The association of the eye of Horus with the faculty of inner sight needs no elucidation and, from the information available concerning this particular symbol, the occultist will have little trouble in realizing that the combined rays of Horus and Bast are excellent for all sorts of healing and regeneration. These eyes came in all shapes and sizes but were usually gold with a blue pupil. It is interesting to note that, although the Egyptians must have been overall a dark-skinned people and therefore predominantly brown-eyed, they almost always depicted their Sun gods with blue eyes. A folk memory, no doubt, of a fair and blue-eyed people who, to them, were the original race of 'gods'. In magical workings the eye is a protective symbol and used, as in the legend, for chasing away one's enemies.

The Djed or Tet
This symbol is also sacred to Osiris. It actually represents a stylized tree and not a phallus as is sometimes thought. It is the emblem of stability and the four cross sections, again, stand for the elemental forces, but this time as manifest in matter and all things solid. It is a good emblem or instrument for the magician who is well acquainted with the gnome kingdoms and has control over his or her material affairs. In instrumental form it should be small and slim in construction, eight inches being considered long enough. For standing purposes it can be much smaller, or in art work it can be used as the dominant picture over the altar. It should be carved in wood, preferably light in colour and without artificial stain. If any colour is used it must be green, but a deeper shade than that associated with the Nephthian rites. The djed should not be confused with the thyrsus, a

staff surmounted by a pine cone, the traditional symbol of Dionysus, in spite of later Greek inclination to consider similarities between the two deities.

The Ankh

Probably the best known of all Egyptian symbols, it can be used as a wand, ornament, or personal adornment. These days ankhs appear in all colours, shapes and sizes, but for magical purposes they should be between twelve and eighteen inches in length, the loop and handle equally balanced, and constructed either of a pure metal or painted in clear sky/turquoise blue, yellow or white. The practitioner who likes to work in natural fibres can use a plain wooden one, but again it must be unstained unless painted in one of the prescribed shades. We are told from psychic sources that in Atlantean times the sacred metal for the ankh was orichalcum, a type of orange-gold no longer known here and mined only in the 'old country'. Bronze is a good ankh metal, although it tends to be weighty. It is in its context as the key of life that it has become popular in recent times, particularly among young people.

The Caduceus

In his *Dictionary of Symbols* Senor Cirlot, the eminent Spanish occultist, writes:

> A wand with two serpents twined round it, surmounted by two small wings or a winged helmet. The rational and historical explanation is the supposed intervention of Mercury in a fight between two serpents who thereupon curled themselves round his wand. For the Romans, the caduceus served as a symbol of moral equilibrium and of good conduct. The wand represents power; the two snakes wisdom; the wings diligence; and the helmet is an emblem of lofty thoughts. Today the caduceus is the insignia of the Catholic bishop in the Ukraine. The caduceus also signifies the integration of the four elements, the wand corresponding to earth, the wings to air, the serpents to fire and water (by analogy with the undulating movement of waves and flames). This symbol is very ancient and is to be found for example in India engraved upon stone tablets called *nâgakals*, a kind of votive offering placed at the entrance to temples. Heinrich Zimmer traces the caduceus back to Mesopotamia, detecting it in the design of the sacrificial cup of king Gudea of Lagash

(2600 B.C.). Zimmer even goes so far as to state that the symbol probably dates back beyond this period, for the Mesopotamians considered the intertwining serpents as the symbol of the god who cures all illness, a meaning which passed into Greek culture and is still preserved in emblems of our day. According to esoteric Buddhism the wand of the caduceus corresponds to the axis of the world and the serpents refer to the force called Kundalini which, in Tantrist teaching, sleeps coiled up at the base of the backbone – a symbol of the evolutive power of pure energy. Schneider maintains that the two S-shapes of the serpents correspond to illness and convalescence. In reality, what defines the essence of the caduceus is the nature and meaning not so much of its individual elements as of the composite whole. The precisely symmetrical and bilateral arrangement, as in the balance of Libra, or in the tri-unity of heraldry (a shield between two supporters), is always expressive of the same idea of active equilibrium, of opposing forces balancing one another in such a way as to create a higher, static form. In the caduceus this balanced duality is twice stated: in the serpents and in the wings, thereby emphasizing that supreme state of strength and self-control (and consequently of health) which can be achieved both on the lower plane of the instincts (symbolized by the serpents) and on the higher level of the spirit (represented by the wings).

The connections with Thoth are obvious, which makes this an ideal wand for any student venturing into the magical service of the 'thrice greatest one'. But care should be taken to ensure that the serpents cross at four points, symbolizing the four elements, and not three times as in some portrayals of this symbol. The caduceus is a 'must' for any Egyptian healing sanctuary. Thoth, together with Horus and Bast, are the main healing deities in the Egyptian system.

The Scarab

The scarab, or sacred beetle, appeared in many forms throughout the Egyptian culture and it is well to understand its significance. It was believed that it was self-produced and, according to old Egyptian folklore, the male beetle wishing to procreate sought out a piece of ox-dung which he shaped into a ball, rolling it from east to west with his hind legs. The ball was then buried in a hole specially dug and left for twenty-eight days. On the twenty-ninth day the beetle threw the dung into the water and the young emerged. Just as life emerged from the ball of dung, so it was believed that all life sprang from the Sun which also moved from east to west. The idea appealed to a simple people and soon became established as a valid religious analogy. Scarabs were worn by priests and people alike and appeared in the representations of many divinities, notably those with solar overtones.

The Lotus
Although generally accepted as a far-eastern symbol, the lotus was used extensively in early Egypt, appearing mainly in scenes depicting the throne of Osiris and the four sons of Horus and was one of the sacred symbols of Nephthys in her role as goddess of mysticism and repose. It carries roughly the same connotations in the Egyptian system as it does in the Indian sub-continent, which speaks for its antiquity.

The Buckle of Isis
A stylized knot or buckle that was usually carved in carnelian. Because of its obvious resemblance to the Yoni it carries strong fertility connotations, while the knot or buckle aspect is indicative of the binding quality of self-sacrifice that usually accompanies the nurturing instinct.

Animal Emblems
For the Egyptians these were just as important as human or abstract symbols and their god-forms were frequently shown with animal features. The lion is a good symbol, so are the cat and dog. As for the wilder beasts, it is all a question of how close an affinity one might feel for, say, a hippopotamus, crocodile or baboon. As many of these concepts crept in from sources other than the one from which the enlightened teaching would appear to have hailed, it is again a matter of sorting the wheat from the chaff. A well-illustrated copy of *The Book of the Dead* will supply the student with a vast amount of symbolism from which he can choose emblems appropriate to his own magical inclinations or cosmic roots.

There are numerous other symbols associated with the Egyptian magical system and the old culture generally. A detailed knowledge of these is not essential to the aspiring magician, and the hieroglyphic vocabulary can be added to as one goes along if

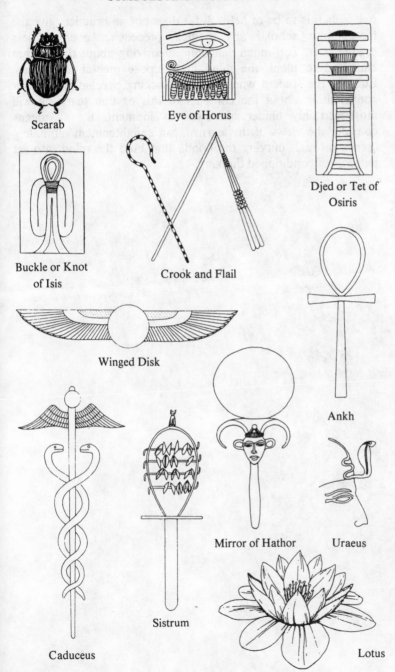

Scarab

Eye of Horus

Djed or Tet of Osiris

Buckle or Knot of Isis

Crook and Flail

Winged Disk

Ankh

Caduceus

Sistrum

Mirror of Hathor

Uraeus

Lotus

one feels this to be of help. But it does not, in practice, give the hieroglyphic scholar any magical precedence over his less erudite peer. Too much academic theorizing about this or that can tend to block the mind and impose mental limitations. Equally, the student who is always seeking psychic answers or confirmation about the contents of this or that textbook will most certainly hinder his own development. By all means consider the views of the learned, but enlightenment ultimately comes through untying the bonds that bind the mind into set patterns of conditioned thinking.

12. COLOURS, ROBES AND ARCHETYPES

In Egyptian ritual magic it is customary for the participants to assume the role of a god or goddess in order to attract the related energies, much after the style of sympathetic magic. For those who like to robe up for their magical practices, a working knowledge of Egyptian occult apparel is essential. Here, to start with, is a list of associated colours, numbers and metals:

Deity	Number	Metallic Colour	Colours
Osiris	1	Deep gold	White and mid green
Isis	2	Pale gold	Clear sky blue
Horus	3	Yellow gold	Bright, clear yellow
Bast	4	Yellow gold	Turquoise
Thoth	5	Silver	Amethystine shades
Hathor	6	Copper	Apricot/coral hues
Nephthys	7	Silver	Pale green/grey green
Ptah	8	Red gold	Violet
Anubis	9	Silver	Terracotta

The colours and metallic shades should be strictly adhered to. For example, in addition to a predominance of the terracotta colour in his robes the representative of Anubis should have all jewellery, temple slippers, embroidery etc. in silver and not mix in gold simply because the fancy takes him.

Head-dresses or head-bands are part of the regalia and should also follow the metallic colour of the god-form. Unless a high degree of initiation has been attained, these should be plain and unornamented. Emblems of occult advancement can be displayed in the headwear, i.e., the uraeus, star, utchat etc., or a simple stone as inspired by the tutelary god or goddess. In fact, much of what is added to the apparel in the way of symbolic ornamentation will be received as inspiration during the course of the proceedings, as this school of magic is by no means a set and rigid one; how one progresses within it will depend very much upon the courage and creative imagination of the aspirant.

The symbol of the represented deity should always be displayed somewhere in the apparel, either suspended around the neck, embroidered in the cloth, worn around the waist, wrist or head etc. If you feel you would like to follow Isis but can't stand the colour blue, your archetype will be wrongly chosen; you might be better off with Hathor or Nephthys. Special footwear should always be kept for ritual magic work. Simple slip-ons of the kind that can be folded up are a good idea. These are usually available in silver or gilt shades and should match the colour of the head-band and any other jewellery worn as appropriate to the rays or archetypes to be employed. As with all magical proceedings, it is advisable to keep paraphernalia securely locked up to ensure that it is not used for any other purposes. Cleanliness, both physical and mental, is essential at all times. The Egyptian priests of old were extremely fastidious about this and would fast, meditate, and then take a long cleansing bath before a working. Never allow children or curious members of the family (or friends) to handle your magical clothing or ritual instruments; it could cause problems during your next working if you do. And never attempt a working if someone within the group is out of harmony, upset, emotionally unstable or bearing ill-will against anyone else present.

If you are of a mind to construct an altar the colours should accord with the god-forms to be invoked, but the lodge principle is the best method of operation and I shall cover this in some detail in the next chapter. With space at a premium in this day and age it is fully understood that few people can set aside a special room or sanctuary for magical workings. A good substitute is a special box or chest which is otherwise kept cleanly sealed and put safely away from prying eyes. The chest itself then becomes the sanctuary, ark or holder of the sacred robes and instruments and a close protection should be placed around it after each working.

As we have already heard from the writings of Iamblichus, the initiated Egyptian priest always wore white robes. The deity they represented and the insignia of their office appeared in colour and symbol form. For example, a priest or priestess of Osiris would wear over their basic white gown a cloak or stole of gold embroidered in green and bearing the emblazoned symbols of crook and flail or djed. If the healing ability were to be emphasized the utchat would be added and a high priest would wear the raised uraeus on his forehead, either in head-band or mitre form. A priestess or priest of Bast would wear a jewelled replica of the sistrum, probably on a neckchain, and also the aegis (a small shield emblazoned with the head of a lion, a reminder that Bast can snarl when she wishes), a basket or cornucopia (bounty), the eye of Horus or the uraeus. (Bast was strongly associated with the uraeus, on account of her defeat of the serpent Apep in the service of Ra.)

The servants of Ptah always wore the masonic cord, which was knotted in a special way around the waist; the colour of this cord varied with the rank and those versed in modern freemasonry could add a few remarks here, no doubt.

Those devoted to the service of Thoth should favour amethystine shades, with the caduceus as the predominant symbol. I have deliberately omitted the Imhotep character from the Memphis triad because his faculty is adequately covered by that of his teacher and master, Thoth. As principal god of medicine, books and the Akasha, the mantle of Thoth can be safely assumed by anyone working along side-channels emanating from this particular archetype, i.e., Imhotep, Khonsu, Nefertum or any of the lesser gods or godlings ascribed to the medical or literary arts.

Animal masks were popular among the priesthood during certain epochs in the Egyptian magical past. Healer priests of Anubis specializing in anaesthetics or embalming, for example, were seen to be going about their tasks wearing an Anubis-type head-piece. But obviously this was shed when they got down to the nitty-gritty; its use in the first place was mainly to give the patient (in the case of healing) the idea that the god himself, and not just his priest, was about to do his stuff. Ibis heads were sacred to Thoth just as Hathor is shown with the head of a cow. Sometimes god-forms are depicted as the complete animal, but this was not the case in the original teachings it would seem.

Many readers may wonder, at this point, why I have mentioned only nine god-forms. My main reason is that I have tried to go right back to the originals and shed as many as possible of the superimpositions and overleaves that crept in during the centuries from the flood to the advent of Christianity. Agreed, I could choose any of the names given in the ennead or even accept the earlier representations of the basic archetypes such as Ra, Geb, Nut, Shu, Tefnut etc.; but I have based my grouping on knowledge gained over many years of actually working with the different rays, experience having shown me that several names, in fact, cover the same identity. I have therefore selected the main archetypes and assigned to them identifiable characteristics that are as close to the Atlantean originals as possible, allowing for human error or the odd psychic misinterpretation or misjudgment. Although it has taken me years of work and study to arrive at these conclusions I by no means write *ex cathedra*, so it is up to every individual to find his or her own way. If he or she should choose to travel via my signposts, then may my meagre notes be of some help. The Trismegistic school favours a return to the Atlantean originals, as will be obvious to the reader, but there are bound to be those among you who will prefer the fundamentalist approach as laid out in the Theban Recension of *The Book of the Dead*, so I shall be covering some of these themes in a later chapter.

Using my method, and that of the Hermetic school, I will briefly outline a few of the principles associated with each of the god-forms I have recommended for magical practices:

Deity	Esoteric Archetype	Mundane Expression
Osiris	King/priest/father	Nature, growth and stability
Isis	High priestess, mistress of magic	Mother and protectress
Horus	Saviour/Sun god/lord of art and music, healer. Twin of Bast	Warrior/oracle/avenger. Patron of the family and home
Bast	Intuition, mental healing, generosity. Twin of Horus	Patroness of marriage, song and dance and the animal kingdoms
Thoth	Scribe to the gods, lord of Akasha, medicine and all academics	All down to earth applications of his esoteric attributes
Hathor	The nourisher and giver of strength	The culinary arts, beauty care for women, love and romance
Nephthys	The revealer/goddess of the intuitive faculty	Servant and supporter, giver of dreams and tranquillity
Ptah	Architect of the universe, divine mason	Science, invention, all work of an artisan nature requiring manual skills
Anubis	Guide/explorer and divine jester	Finder of lost things, protector of the traveller, navigator, diplomat

The gift of prophecy is traditionally associated with Horus and Nephthys; physical strength with Horus and Hathor; healing with Thoth, Horus and Bast; magic with Isis and Thoth; legal and governmental matters with Thoth and Osiris, and the more mundane things of life with Anubis, Hathor and Ptah.

13. THE STRUCTURE OF THE LODGE OR GROUP

When working Egyptian magic it is advisable to keep to a regular group or lodge, so the utmost care should be taken to gather together people who are in harmony at the spiritual, mental and physical levels. The psychic person chosen as scryer should be able to scan the time zones for the lodge master to ensure that those selected have similar or harmoniously related karmic backgrounds. The Egyptian discipline does not suit everyone and some systems are more in tune with it than others. If you are of Pagan, Norse, Wiccan or Celtic inclination you might find it easier to accommodate the Egyptian frequency than if you were primarily drawn to, say, the Buddhic, Semitic or Christian mystical traditions. But then again it will depend on when and where in the past your spirit underwent its occult introductions.

The Egyptian working group or lodge should consist of no more than nine and preferably several less, the ideal number being five. It should always include the following roles:

Celebrant Hierophant (the lodge master)
Scryer
Keeper
Protector
Recorder

Other roles may be added according to the god-forms assumed.

The celebrant should always handle the elemental evocations and altar work. The protector is responsible for keeping up a continual guard during the working and also ensuring that all conditions and disciplines are correctly observed prior to commencement. It is the duty of the scryer to 'look in' when so requested by the celebrant, who will hand him or her the chalice containing clear water for this purpose. Each session must be noted by the recorder, who is also responsible for marking down later developments that may result from workings undertaken. The keeper is responsible for the maintenance of the magical instruments and for the correct setting up of the altar etc.

When a group of people decide to form an Egyptian lodge the foundation should be correctly effected. A propitious astrological date should be chosen and the lodge 'initiated', on the inner planes (etherically) in the first instance, before any workings take place. According to how this initiation 'takes' the lodge master will know roughly what course his or her lodge is likely to follow. It should be borne in mind that the world of magic is *not* a democracy and positions should always be allocated according to specific attributes and *not* popularity. The best scryer may not be the prettiest, or the best lodge leader the easiest. But if they are suited for the task, then that is that.

Having established the order it is essential for the smooth working of the lodge that a discipline is adhered to. Magical working sessions are *not* debating panels and if this sort of thing creeps in the lodge will soon fold up. People seeking to air their personal views or slip in the odd ego trip should avoid Egyptian magic completely and confine their talents to a debating society. If a dissatisfaction should arise it should be taken immediately to the lodge master and his or her decision supported. If that decision is not acceptable to the dissenter, then he should leave the lodge and make way for another who is more harmonious with the group. If a lodge is disbanded, this should be done with full closing ritual, the energy lines sealed and the auras of the participants securely closed down and severed from the lodge umbilical.

Any occultist of experience reading this will no doubt remark that these are rules that apply to all lodges in all systems, which is so in many cases, but the dangers of not keeping within cosmic laws when working this system are, in my experience, considerably greater. Perhaps this is because the energies that can be tapped are also finer, more subtle and, therefore, more unstable. It takes a disciplined mind to cope with the abstract and Egyptian magic deals an awful lot with the 'unmanifest'.

Each member within a lodge should assume a god-form, according to his or her own nature and type. Certain god-forms belong to the celebrant class, i.e., Osiris, Isis and Thoth; the scryer god-forms are Nephthys and Horus; the keeper arche-types are Bast, Ptah and Anubis; the protectors are Hathor and Horus; and the recorders are Thoth and Osiris. When all nine god-forms are employed each can assume the specific god-role as given in the last chapter. It is possible to interchange some of the roles, however; Bast can protect as can Isis, Anubis can record as can Ptah; and so forth.

Having carefully selected the god-form, each member should 'become' the archetype in his or her own mind during workings and endeavour to imbibe the nature and attributes thereof. The colours representing the god-forms should be mentally absorbed and then radiated out to join with the others at a centre point in the grouping, so that the celebrant can take each strand and weave them all into a rainbow pattern. The colours, if they are correctly handled, should harmonize perfectly. Any blur will highlight an area of deficiency, which could either involve an incorrect selection on the part of one member or an evolutionary (spiritual generation gap) imbalance among those present. If this is not adjusted as soon as possible someone will suffer.

All lodge workings should be correctly opened and securely closed and participants should be sure to 'earth' properly afterwards. This can be achieved either through a disciplined session of the 'body-consciousness' type, i.e., becoming aware of one's toes, ankles, knees, thighs etc., consciously closing one's aura or ritually earthing via the gnome kingdoms. No hard and fast rules here; it is up to the lodge master as to what he or she feels to be best for those under his or her care.

It must be appreciated that group and lodge structures have altered considerably over the centuries. Traditionalists wishing to keep in line with established procedures should look to the fomulae adhered to by orders such as the Knights Templars, or any of the masonic-type cults with Egyptian overtones. Isian rites in Graeco-Roman times are well covered by Dr R.A. Witt in his excellent book *Isis in the Graeco-Roman World*. Seasonal ceremonies such as the procession to the ship are easy to follow through in this day and age and would doubtless appeal to the younger generation who are more cosmically minded. The Egyptian system also abounded with public ceremonies which usually ended up in a carnival atmosphere with everybody having a good time; but a hint of warning here: the serious magical aspects were always dealt with in private by the priests prior to opening the festivities to the public. So, if you aim to have a ball after your working, be sure to close all occult doors securely and simply treat the enjoyment period as you would a normal 'earthing'. Any group or society wishing to pursue Egyptian religious practices that involve the public should keep things on a fairly low key occultly and forces should not be invoked that might possibly cause discomfort or embarrassment to the uninitiated. There is plenty to draw from on the lighter side and Dr Witt's work provides an excellent source of safe information in this direction.

There are many misconceptions regarding the roles of occultist, scryer/psychic, mystic etc., and I would refer those who are unsure as to which is what to my book *Practical Techniques of Psychic Self Defence* (Aquarian Press) in which I give clear definitions. It is essential for the student of Egyptian occultism to understand these initially, because the lines of demarcation become very blurred when one is working in abstract magic. For example, the lodge may initiate a working in which help or power is invoked for a specific cause of light, i.e., to assist people in trouble, to alleviate suffering, to bring peace and harmony or to render healing. Not only could the energies invoked be released through the working, but the gods may also see fit to show those present why the condition arose in the first place. This could involve intuitive flashes of past lives, former historical situations, or even the reception of a 'teaching' or philosophy designed to counteract the problem and possibly prevent it from recurring. So, in addition to directive magic, the receptive side has to be coped with and the lodge could find itself with a mine of information that it doesn't quite know how to handle.

This system brings knowledge and wisdom but it does not require a soap-box, so those who like to shun publicity of any kind need not feel guilty if they don't spread the word around. In fact, it might be wiser if they didn't. Knowledge may be bestowed simply to give them, as individuals, a better understanding of what they are doing and its effects, no matter how small, on the times in which they live and the evolution of the planet generally. So, Egyptian lodge master, keep a balance in your 'house' between the positive or directive aspects of magic and the receptive and intuitional sides: Osiris/Thoth, Horus/ Nephthys. Dwell too much on either side and an imbalance will ensue.

It is not advisable to have a lodge or group that is all male or all female. A balance is ideal and, if some of the couples at least are natural polarities, then all the better. Twin souls working this system will draw a considerable amount of power as they will have access to the 'twin-source', i.e., Sirius, but I will deal with that in a later chapter. It is unlikely that a genuine twinning will occur, however, as this is rare anyway and only takes place in the later stages of 'old soul' development.

Domestic animals were allowed to sit in at Egyptian temple workings in olden times, providing they were temple trained, and the same applies today. An undisciplined animal can cause disturbance, especially to a scryer, but a quiet creature can prove a great help. Animals have also had their former lives (or existence in other time zones, as I prefer to say) and your cat might well have been trained in the temples of Bast or Sekhmet, or the Tibetan orders in which these animals guard the sacred scrolls. I have personally found cats to be extremely good protectors against the lower astral, but one cannot generalize and it all depends on the nature of the beast. One of my cats is high spirited and becomes extremely excited when the atmosphere is raised during a magical working. The other two, on the contrary, immediately vacate their bodies and keep up a dedicated 'watchdog' routine, only to wake again when all has been closed up.

If you are an occultist trained to work with the velocia (tattvic tides), by all means incorporate this into the Egyptian system. Remember, however, that each deity has an affinity with a definite element and, if you decide to employ these intervals, it is well to observe the elemental kinships if you wish to obtain the best and most harmonious results.

Learning by heart or 'swotting up' on a few rituals and then relying on them does not guarantee results with Egyptian rites. The discipline of ritual and the devotional aspects are all very fine and uplifting, but sooner or later you will reach a stage where you find yourself alone and thrown back on your own creative imagination. So much work in this system is carried out while out of the body that one needs to be a firm friend of Anubis to start with. Remember, he is lord of all out of the body experiences, both voluntary and involuntary. He is a great help, incidentally, when one is undergoing a surgical operation under anaesthetics; I can personally vouch for that, as can several of my friends.

The Egyptians had two teachings, one for the outer temple or worshipping public and one for the inner temple or priesthood. During the history of Egypt successive generations of spiritually sightless persons usurped the position of the true priesthood and the structure slowly collapsed. Temporal power does not mix with the true gifts of priesthood and, when any ecclesiastical establishment starts playing a political game, the decline sets in, as may be evidenced throughout the pages of history. It is as well to bear in mind Eliphas Levi's famous statement: 'Magic is not a profession.'

14. SUGGESTIONS AND WARNINGS

Before tackling the practical applications of the Egyptian system it is as well to devote a few paragraphs to a consideration of what it is and what it is not. A few cautionary words are also in order.

It is not an exact system with set formulae and guaranteed results. On the other hand it has definite rights and wrongs and, if one adopts an inaccurate way of working, it will either misfire completely or the results will be nil. As with all role-playing magical systems, a knowledge of the part enacted by the archetype in the celestial hierarchy helps to highlight the roles of its participants in the drama of life. To know oneself in relation to the drama is to know the unfoldment of one's karma. The scene can be set in any period of history but the characters are the same. The god-nature exists within each of us; we are gods in the making and identification with the principles they represent can only help us towards the knowledge and understanding they embrace at their higher octaves. The gods need, therefore, to be recognized and their principles mastered within ourselves, which means there is no quick and easy access to power by way of Egyptiana.

As has been commented in previous chapters, the old Egyptian philosophy did not accommodate the eastern concept that everything evolves through the kingdoms of lesser consciousness, its experience finally culminating in the *Homo sapiens* form. The view was rather that different species evolved in separate streams, with certain planets or star systems affording conditions conducive to the development of a refined intellect and sensitive state of consciousness. If we burned our fingers as a child we would be able to recall the pain and use that recollection to avoid repeating the discomfort. Experience tempers understanding, be it conscious or subconscious. Had we evolved from the flower that stretches forth its petals to the Sun, the gnome that fashioned the amethystine crystals or the animal seeking food for its young, we would never deliberately tread on a bloom, uproot a young tree, pollute the earth or hunt for pleasure, unless we were mentally sick. Can a gentle and loving animal, by assuming a human form, become bestial and cruel? All these answers and many others will quickly come to those who seek according to the Egyptian path.

Although mankind is the dominant species here on Earth, there is no guarantee of his dominance in other parts of the universe. Furthermore, because the cat, dog, plant or gnome are in what might appear to be a submissive and less consciously developed mode, this does not deny them the right to attain to an intellectually equal or even superior position to *Homo sapiens* in some other part of the cosmos.

Bearing these remarks in mind, it would be inadvisable for anyone to delve into the Egyptian system with the preconceived notion that man is of some supreme intellectually developed order designed by the deity to give the orders. Much as the idea may flatter your ego, and brainwashed into it though you may be, it won't take you anywhere in the Egyptian study. All intelligences at all levels have their own power and, to obtain the best occult results, one must comprehend the nature of that power *by thinking with it* and then working as part of it. This technique is not achieved by the domination mode but rather through two-way absorption.

Let us take for example the four elements, fire, air, water and earth. The Egyptian occult method is to tap their power through *understanding* them. The ability to tune one's thoughts to the thought patterns of a salamander, and thus identify with the brotherhood of fire, will require one to shed false egos acquired over successive epochs of materialistic indoctrination. All things within the cosmos are interrelated and it is only natural for kindred souls to come to the aid of their own kind, especially when threatened from alien or non-harmonious frequencies. The secret lies in being able to become one of that 'kind', whatever it may be, so that you attract its help in time of need. It is said, for example, that he who relates to the gnome kingdoms never wants for a penny.

A few 'don'ts' coming up:

Don't touch Egyptian magic or anything even vaguely connected with it unless you are completely at ease and feel a strong affinity with the animal kingdom.

Don't lean too heavily on ancient texts that have suffered severely in translation over the centuries; what this or that scholar commented about it in the Middle Ages; or even fragments that have supposedly filtered down via tradition. Better to rely upon your own intuition and karmic past. Creative imagination and a quick, adaptable mind are essential prerequisites for success within the Egyptian discipline.

If you are a hedonist or anarchistically inclined, *give up the idea completely*. This magical discipline abides very strictly by cosmic laws and there is none of the 'do as thou wilt' about it when it comes to the practice, however much you may read to the contrary. An acceptance of its principles demands an acknowledgement of the life force in all things. Nothing is here to be abused. Everything merits respect in accordance with its specific design and purpose.

Before you take your first steps sort out your personal and god symbols as these will be your protective codes and active safety devices (see *Practical Techniques of Psychic Self Defence*).

In my experience the occult is something that cannot be taught. There are people who can advise as to the best method of coping with this problem or crossing that bridge or spiritual highway but, in the final analysis, it is between you and the gods, which demands genuine humility at every stage. Nor is it simply a question of will power as so many people are inclined to think. The will to sing does not guarantee one the gift of a voice and the will to be an occultist, mystic or scryer will not ensure the hard working pupil a place in the metaphysical scheme of things. This is why it is so essential to know oneself.

Sometimes the best occultists or psychics are those who spend a lot of their time trying to avoid the issue. They may feel themselves unworthy of such responsibilities, or be anxious for fear of inadvertently causing suffering to another through ignorance or human failing. None of us are perfect and mistakes will occur along the line. The wise and brave soul is the one who picks himself up, dusts himself down, rubs his bruises and carries on. Resilience is an essential psychological ingredient in the make-up of the good occultist.

When it comes to the question of converting the abstract into concrete terms of Earth reference our brains can only be programmed to accept so much at a time. Keep within that limit, carry on your ordinary day-to-day life, without neglecting your worldly duties, and you will find in the old Egyptian gods some firm and reliable friends.

15. ANCIENT PRAYERS AND INVOCATIONS

Although *The Book of the Dead* concerns itself primarily with the state of the soul after death, various magical procedures are also featured. One of the most potent forms of Egyptian magic was concerned with the name or identity. To become familiar with the names of the gods was most important and this did not simply mean their popular earthly nomenclatures. In fact, the name cult grew to such outlandish proportions as to be ridiculous, the petitioner often being required to memorize lists upon lists of obscure and meaningless titles. In magical practice the inscriptions used were of the utmost importance, also the manner of approaching the deity. For those who like to work directly from old texts, here are a few examples.

The first is a hymn and litany to Osiris from the *Papyrus of Ani* (British Museum No. 10470, sheet 19). The original is accompanied by a vignette, depicting the scribe himself and a singing woman holding a sistrum. The text goes:

> Praise be unto thee, O Osiris, lord of eternity, Un-nefer, Heru-Khuti (Harmachis), whose forms are manifold, and whose attributes are majestic, Ptah-Seker-Tem in Annu (Heliopolis), the lord of the hidden place, and the creator of Het-ka-Ptah and of the gods (therein), the guide of the underworld, whom (the gods) glorify when thou settest in Nut. Isis embraceth thee in peace, and she driveth away the fiends from the mouth of thy paths. Thou turnest thy face upon Amentet, and thou makest the earth to shine as with

refined copper. Those who have lain down (i.e., the dead) rise up to see thee, they breathe the air and they look upon thy face when the disk riseth on its horizon; their hearts are at peace inasmuch as they behold thee, O thou who art Eternity and Everlastingness!

LITANY

1. *Petition.* – Homage to thee, (O lord of) starry deities in Annu, and of heavenly beings in Kher-aha; thou god Unti, who art more glorious than the gods who are hidden in Annu.

Response. – O grant thou unto me a path whereon I may pass in peace, for I am just and true; I have not spoken lies wittingly, nor have I done aught with deceit.

2. *Petition.* – Homage to thee, O An in Antes (?), Heru-khuti (Harmachis), with long strides thou stridest over heaven, O Heru-khuti.

Response. – O grant thou unto me a path whereon I may pass in peace, for I am just and true etc. (The same response is repeated in litanical fashion after each petition.)

3. *Petition.* – Homage to thee, O Soul of everlastingness, thou Soul that dwellest in Tattu, Un-nefer, son of Nut; thou art lord of Akert.

Response.

4. *Petition.* – Homage to thee in thy dominion over Tattu; the *Ureret* crown is established upon thy head; thou art the one who maketh the strength which protecteth himself, and thou dwellest in peace in Tattu.

Response.

5. *Petition.* – Homage to thee, O lord of the Acacia Tree, the *Seker* boat is set upon its sledge; thou turnest back the Fiend, the worker of evil, and thou causest the *Utchat* to rest upon its seat.

Response.

6. *Petition.* – Homage to thee, O thou who art mighty in thine hour, thou great and mighty Prince, dweller in An-rut-f, lord of eternity and creator of everlastingness, thou art the lord of Suten-henen.

Response.

7. *Petition.* – Homage to thee, O thou who restest upon Right and Truth, thou art the lord of Abtu (Abydos) and thy limbs art joined unto Ta-tchesertet; thou art he to whom fraud and guile are hateful.

Response.

8. *Petition.* – Homage to thee, O thou who art within thy boat, thou bringest Hapi (i.e., the Nile) forth from his source; the light shineth upon thy body and thou art the dweller in Nekhen.

Response.

9. *Petition.* – Homage to thee, O creator of the gods, thou King of the North and of the South, O Osiris, victorious one, ruler of the world in thy gracious seasons; thou art the lord of the celestial world.

Response.

This type of prayer is not unlike the litanies of certain Christian sects today. It can be fitted into a ritual magical working in which the Osirian group of gods are to be featured or simply used by two people working together, with one speaking the petition and the other the response.

My next quote will doubtless be of interest to those who find themselves fascinated by the Sirius school of magic, as direct reference is made to the twinning so important in that system. The first few stanzas are from the *Papyrus of Ani* (British Museum Ref. No. 10470, sheets 7-10) and the remaining lines from the *Papyrus of Nebseni* (British Museum No. 9900, sheet 14,1. 16ff).

(Ani) 'I am the divine Soul which dwelleth in the divine Twin-Gods.'

What then is this?

It is Osiris (when) he goeth into Tattu and findeth there the soul of Ra; there the one god embraceth the other, and divine souls spring into being within the divine Twin-Gods.

(Nebseni) As concerning the divine Twin-Gods they are Heru-netch-hra-tef-f and Heru-khent-an-maati; or (as others say) the double divine Soul which dwelleth in the divine Twin-Gods is the Soul of Ra and the Soul of Osiris; (or (as others say),) it is the Soul which dwelleth in Shu, (and) the Soul which dwelleth in Tefnut, and these are the double divine Soul which dwelleth in Tattu.

'I am the Cat which fought (?) hard by the Persea tree in Annu (Heliopolis), on the night when the foes of Neb-er-tcher were destroyed.'

Who then is this?

The male Cat is Ra himself, and he is called 'Mau' by reason of the speech of the god Sa, (who said) concerning him: 'He is like *(mau)* unto that which he hath made'; thus his name became 'Mau'; or (as others say) it is the god Shu who maketh over the possessions of Seb to Osiris.

As concerning the fight (?) hard by the Persea tree in Annu, it concerneth the children of impotent revolt when justice is wrought on them for what they have done.

As concerning the night of the battle (these words refer to) the inroad (of the children of impotent revolt) into the eastern part of heaven, whereupon there arose a battle in heaven and in all the earth.

'Oh thou who art in thine egg (i.e., Ra) who shinest from thy Disk and risest in thy horizon, and dost shine like gold above the sky, like unto whom there is none among the gods, who sailest over the pillars of Shu (i.e., in the ether), who givest blasts of fire from thy mouth, (who makest the two lands bright with thy radiance, deliver) thou the pious Nebseni from the god whose form is hidden, whose eyebrows are like unto the two arms of the Balance on the night of reckoning destruction . . .' etc.

The aforegoing serves as a first class example of how the same gods were known by many names. The twin lion gods, Shu and Tefnut, appear in different guises throughout the Egyptian pantheon, emerging latterly as Horus and Bast, in which aspects I have chosen to employ them in my own magical usage. Over the centuries the lion assumed the calmer form of the cat, possibly to distinguish her from the more forceful Sekhmet, which is Hathor's warrior *persona* and not actually a separate divinity. Another suggestion made to me was that, in the 'old country', certain tame lions were kept as domestic pets and particularly favoured by the judiciary who tended to keep them nearby during legal hearings.

The Negative Confession
The *Papyrus of Nebseni* gives a fine example of the famous judgment scene where the soul of the departed is required to give forty-two statements of all the merits it has achieved during its lifetime (or all the wrongs it did not commit). This is too lengthy a document to reproduce in its entirety, but it is worthy of inclusion as many who subscribe to the old methods of Egyptian magical practice are of the opinion that this, or a shortened version, should be recited prior to invoking the gods, either as a form of banishing ritual or to reassure the deities whose attentions are being sought that the suppliant is of righteous and honest intent.

The original papyrus was, as always with that period, accompanied by a vignette, an explanation of which seems an appropriate introduction to the ensuing texts from the *Papyrus of Nebseni* (British Museum No. 9900, sheet 30):

Vignette: The Hall of double Maati, that is to say the Hall of the goddesses Isis and Nephthys who symbolize Right and Truth; herein are seated or stand forty-two gods, to each of whom the deceased must address a prescribed negative statement. At each end is one half of a folding door, one having the name of Neb-

Maat-heri-tep-retui-f and the other of Neb-pehti-Qesu-menmenet. On the centre of the roof, which has a cornice of uraei, typifying divinity, and feathers, symbolic of Maat, is a seated deity, painted bluish-green, with hands extended, the right over the Eye of Horus, and the left over a pool. At the end of the Hall are four small vignettes, in which are depicted: 1. The Maati goddesses, each seated upon a throne and holding a sceptre in her right hand, and the emblem of life in her left. 2. The deceased, arrayed in white, standing before the god Osiris with both hands raised in adoration. 3. A balance with the heart, symbolizing the conscience of the deceased, in one scale, and the feather, emblematic of Right and Truth, in the other. The god Anubis is testing the tongue of the balance, and close by stands the monster Am-met. 4. Thoth, ibis-headed, seated upon a pylon-shaped pedestal, painting a large feather of Maat. In the Papyrus of Anhai the gods are seated in a double row; each has his characteristic head, and nearly all wear the feather of Maat.

Text: The scribe Nebseni, triumphant, saith:

1. 'Hail, thou whose strides are long, who comest forth from Annu (Heliopolis), I have not done iniquity.
2. Hail, thou who art embraced by flame, who comest forth from Kher-aha, I have not robbed with violence.
3. Hail, thou divine Nose (Fenti), who comest forth from Khemennu (Hermopolis), I have not done violence (to any man).
4. Hail, thou who eatest shades, who comest forth from the place where the Nile riseth, I have not committed theft.
5. Hail, Neha-hau, who comest forth from Re-stau, I have not slain man or woman.
6. Hail, thou double Lion-god, who comest forth from heaven, I have not made light the bushel.
7. Hail, thou whose two eyes are like flint, who comest forth from Sekhem (Letopolis), I have not acted deceitfully.
8. Hail, thou Flame, who comest forth as (thou) goest back, I have not purloined the things which belong unto God.
9. Hail, thou Crusher of bones, who comest forth from Suten-henen (Hera-cleopolis), I have not uttered falsehood.
10. Hail, thou who makest the flame to wax strong, who comest forth from Het-ka-Ptah (Memphis), I have not carried away food.
11. Hail, Qerti (i.e., the two sources of the Nile), who come forth from Amentet, I have not uttered evil words.
12. Hail, thou whose teeth shine, who comest forth from Ta-she (i.e. the Fayyum), I have attacked no man.
13. Hail, thou who dost consume blood, who comest forth from the

house of slaughter, I have not killed the beasts (which are the property of God).

14. Hail, thou who dost consume the entrails, who comest forth from the *mabet* chamber, I have not acted deceitfully.

15. Hail, thou god of Right and Truth, who comest forth from the city of double Maati, I have not laid waste the lands which have been ploughed (?).

16. Hail, thou who goest backwards, who comest forth from the city of Bast (Bubastis), I have never pried into matters (to make mischief).

17. Hail, Aati, who comest forth from Annu (Heliopolis), I have not set my mouth in motion (against any man).

18. Hail, thou who art doubly evil, who comest forth from the nome of Ati, I have not given way to wrath concerning myself without a cause.

19. Hail, thou serpent Uamenti, who comest forth from the house of slaughter, I have not defiled the wife of a man.

20. Hail, thou who lookest upon what is brought to him, who comest forth from the Temple of Amsu, I have not committed any sin against purity.

21. Hail, Chief of the divine Princes, who comest forth from the city of Nehatu, I have not struck fear (into any man).

22. Hail, Khemi (i.e., Destroyer), who comest forth from the Lake of Kaul (Khas?), I have not encroached upon (sacred times and seasons).

23. Hail, thou who orderest speech, who comest forth from Urit, I have not been a man of anger.

24. Hail, thou Child, who comest forth from the Lake of Heq-at, I have not made myself deaf to the words of right and truth.

25. Hail, thou disposer of speech, who comest forth from the city of Unes, I have not stirred up strife.

26. Hail, Basti, who comest forth from the Secret city, I have made no (man) to weep.

27. Hail, thou whose face is (turned) backwards, who comest forth from the Dwelling, I have not committed acts of impurity, neither have I lain with men.

28. Hail, Leg of fire, who comest forth from Akhekhu, I have not eaten my heart.

29. Hail, Kenemti, who comest forth from (the city of) Kenemet, I have abused (no man).

30. Hail, thou who bringest thine offering, who comest forth from the city of Sau (Sais), I have not acted with violence.

31. Hail, thou lord of faces, who comest forth from the city of Tchefet, I have not judged hastily.

32. Hail, thou who givest knowledge, who comest forth from Unth, I

have not . . ., and I have not taken vengeance upon the god.

33. Hail, thou lord of two horns, who comest forth from Satiu, I have not multiplied (my) speech over-much.

34. Hail, Nefer-Tem, who comest forth from Het-ka-Ptah (Memphis), I have not acted with deceit, and I have not worked wickedness.

35. Hail, Tem-Sep, who comest forth from Tattu, I have not uttered curses (on the king).

36. Hail, thou whose heart doth labour, who comest forth from the city of Tebti, I have not fouled (?) water.

37. Hail, Ahi of the water, who comest forth from Nu, I have not made haughty my voice.

38. Hail, thou who givest commands to mankind, who comest forth from (Sau (?)), I have not cursed the god.

39. Hail, Neheb-nefert, who comest forth from the Lake of Nefer (?), I have not behaved with insolence.

40. Hail, Neheb-kau, who comest forth from (thy) city, I have not sought for distinctions.

41. Hail, thou whose head is holy, who comest forth from (thy) habitation, I have not increased my wealth, except with such things as are (justly) mine own possessions.

42. Hail, thou who bringest thine own arm, who comest forth from Aukert (underworld), I have not thought scorn of the god who is in my city.'

This was traditionally followed by a direct address to the gods of the underworld . . . etc.

Lastly, we have a very popular ritual speech and invocation, also from the Nebseni papyrus, in which Horus addresses his divine father during their meeting in the higher planes. It commences:

I ascribe praise to thee, O lord of the Gods, thou God One, who livest upon right and truth, behold I, thy son Horus, come unto thee; I have avenged thee and I have brought thee *Maat* – even to the place where is the company of the gods. Grant thou that I may have my being among those who are in thy following, for I have overthrown all thy foes, and have stablished all those who are of thy substance upon the earth for ever and ever.

This is followed by forty declarations, each of which is preceded by the words 'Hail, Osiris, I am thy son' and which state the many good deeds, both material and spiritual, that Horus, or the priest/suppliant who is ritually assuming the Horus role, has carried out on behalf of Osiris.

The forty declarations, like so many of these old prayers and rituals, are irrelevant to life today, being concerned with such matters as delivering up the enemies of the god from among conquered people, sacrifices of food, the safety and long life of the reigning monarch etc., which is why it is so important to extract the essence of this magical system and not become bogged down by detail when attempting to get close to first principles. It is important to remember that these texts were ancient when they were copied all those centuries ago, so nobody really has much idea what the originals had to say anyway. One can only try to reach the truth via the psychic or intuitive faculty, with an earnest request to the gods for enlightenment. If one is of right intent one will receive the correct guidance, as like attracts like. Hence the significance of the Negative Confession.

Copies of *The Book of the Dead* can be obtained through the public library system. Doubtless those of sufficient dedication will search round old bookshops and find their own copies; they are not all that difficult to come by. But, all in all, it is best to start from scratch using the correct archetypes rather than to rely upon the rather suspect and highly coloured local translations that are available from historical and archaeological sources.

16. CEREMONIAL MAGIC

The method of procedure is a simple one. Each person participating assumes the role of one of the nine major deities previously outlined. If robing is desired, the apparel must be in keeping with the list supplied in Chapter 12, and the customary altar and sacred instruments will be required if full ceremonial is to be employed. It is *absolutely essential* that any energies invoked or evoked are utilized, otherwise they must be correctly dispersed to their natural frequencies or normal spheres of activity. If you are not sure where those are, the inference is that you had no idea whence you summoned them in the first place, in which case you should *not* be 'dabbling' in Egyptian magic. First get to know your way around the world of the occult, as this is *not* a system for the beginner or experimenter.

Rules and Order of Procedure
Thoroughly prepare the place in which the working is to be held. This may be done with a banishing or cleansing ritual or by pure mind power. The celebrant should arrange the placings well before the commencement of the working and the law of polarity should be as strictly adhered to as possible, i.e., male-female, male-female etc. If the group or lodge finds itself with more of one sex than the other the polarizing should be achieved through the use of the god-forms, with one of the ladies assuming a male god-form or a gentleman taking on a goddess role. A warning here about homosexuality. Popular though it may be to accept

this mode of conduct in modern day society, the Egyptian priests of old disapproved of it; in fact, those of that inclination were banned from temple work. This is *not* the author's judgment, it is simply a statement of the rules laid down in those times.

Incense may be used, preferably sandalwood which blends with all the god-forms, although some may prefer a specialist mixture. This can be burned in stick form or in a thurible as decided by the master.

The ceremony should be ritually opened and closed and *thanks always rendered to any intelligences that have been kind enough to proffer their aid.* Good manners were not the prerogative of the Victorians; the universe and all things in it like to be appreciated.

The lodge keeper should ensure that the altar is correctly laid, with the elemental symbols placed to their appropriate points of the compass. The chalice or cup should contain clear, pure water and the candles should not be lit until everyone is in position for the start of the ceremony. Candles should be coloured according to the nature of the invocation and as decided by the lodge master. If several invocations are planned, then the colour followed through must accord with the role assumed by the celebrant.

Music may be employed, but it should be soft and flowing and *not contain any definite kind of beat.* Beat music is totally out of harmony with Egyptian magic and will have the effect of shifting the power to one or other side of the 'centre', so that it starts to flow into primitive channels which immediately cut out the higher frequencies.

The god-forms specifically invoked should be chosen according to the nature of the request. For example, matters pertaining to literature, knowledge, medicine or time come under the jurisdiction of Thoth. Assuming that the celebrant is not himself assuming the Thoth role, he should call forth the lodge member who is robed for this and address him or her as he would the god. That member should then by-pass the thinking and reasoning hemisphere of his brain and allow the right or intuitional side to take over, so that he can act as a line of communication between the group and the god.

It is the duty of the protector to keep up a full and vigilant guard around the working at all times, commencing well before the start of the ceremony. This protective role should be

atmosphere settled and harmonious.

17. SOME PRACTICAL MAGICAL TECHNIQUES

There are many people who see the occult only in terms of group workings, lodge activities and the like, but the Egyptian system is by no means limited to that field of magical activity. In fact, it lends itself far more to certain specialized techniques, a few of which I will outline. These can be used either with or without ritual.

The Scales of Maat

Purpose. For ascertaining the real intention or purpose behind a proposition or situation. For example, someone offers you a friendship or gift about which you feel strangely uncomfortable, or a situation arises that requires a decision on your part but which you find yourself viewing with a degree of illogical suspicion. The scales of Maat are said to bring the truth of the matter into the open within a 'three', usually three days but sometimes three weeks.

Method. Visualize a pair of scales (or you can work ritually with real scales if you prefer). On the left hand balance place a representation of the problem, i.e., something either symbolic of, or practically related to, the situation. On the right hand balance place the white feather of truth. If you are working through mind magic make a mental picture of yourself raising the scales and handing them to Maat or Thoth. As you do so you will sense them becoming lighter and lighter and rising as though weightless, until they are taken from your hands and gradually disappear into the regions of light above. It is essential to wait until the invoked deity relieves you of your burden, but I have never yet heard of a case when this did not take place almost immediately. Simple, isn't it? Then you just sit back and wait. I first used the scales of Maat many years ago when I was approached by somebody regarding a proposed magical relationship about which I felt uneasy for no valid reason. Within three days the person in question displayed his true colours.

If worked ritually, the scales, set with the feather on one side and some small item that identifies the problem on the other, are offered to Maat with an accompanying prayer. The two items must then be ritually burned and the ashes dispersed to the four points of the compass with due thanks to Maat and the four elements.

The Mirror of Hathor
Of course you will need a Hathor mirror for this and, again, it can be worked with or without ceremonial. I prefer it without ceremonial. As has already been explained, the mirror of Hathor is clear on one side but slightly scoured on the other. When wishing to look in on someone whose intentions you suspect, always employ the clear side; but when rebounding unwelcome or inharmonious vibes back to the sender the scoured side is the one to use.

Purpose. If you feel you are receiving the unwanted attentions of someone with whom you are not in harmony, and who might conceivably be using magical techniques or strong thought forces to get through to you, these can be rebounded onto the sender. Never look directly into the face of anyone you suspect of being an enemy; this applies even more to out of the body experiences than in the traditional, practical meaning. All the old legends proffer this advice; the heroes and godlings of mythological fame inevitably faced their opponents armed with some form of reflective device so that they were not obliged to encounter the direct force of the attack. The clear side of the Hathor mirror also serves as an excellent gateway to the clairvoyant faculty and several people who have developed under my guidance have found it invaluable in this context.

Method. For rebounding unwanted vibes, or as a form of protection against such contingencies, make a mental picture of what you feel to be *the results* of the 'evil eye'. For example, the water system has gone wrong in your house for several days in a row, you have sustained a series of minor accidents through no fault of your own, you have felt utterly drained since spending an hour with a certain person etc. Visualize the relevant situation and, if working in practical ritual, write it down on a clean piece of paper. Then look into the clear side of your mirror, say your prayer to Hathor and at the same time place your problem (either in your mind's eye or using the piece of paper) against the other side *without looking into that side yourself*. Still viewing the clear side and with the scoured side facing outward, raise the mirror as though reflecting back the situation to the sender. Complicated wording is not necessary, a simple statement such as 'I hereby return to the sender all unkind thoughts and evil wishes that have been sent in my direction; may Hathor be my messenger as she was messenger for Ra'. Always end every magical practice with a prayer of thanksgiving, either mentally or verbally, according to your method of working.

Ptah and Craftsmanship

As god of artisans and all forms of construction, Ptah is a most helpful deity, especially when one is faced with what might appear to be an insoluble problem of a manual or mechanical kind. A brief invocation to him at such times is never amiss and again one can carry this out either mentally or ritually. When faced with Ptah-type problem situations, however, one is seldom equipped for an appropriate magical working, as emergencies of this kind inevitably raise their ugly head when one is poised half way up a ladder looking into a complicated fuse box or stuck with an immovable screw. Never be afraid to call upon Ptah in your mind; I have never known him to refuse a sincere plea. The answer usually comes in the form of an idea as to how to solve the problem, but I have personally experienced some strange phenomena when seeking Ptah's aid. On one occasion I was trying to dislodge some masonry in a wall when a whole block of the stuff started to come away. I could have been badly injured as I did not possess the physical strength to contain the onfall. Hastily I beseeched Ptah to aid me and the results were phenomenal. The whole structure seemed to become as light as a feather and slid easily back into position. A gratifying experience and, as the old saying goes, faith can move mountains.

But then I happen to believe in Ptah.

The Protection of Property

In earlier chapters we considered how the Egyptians in ancient times protected their tombs in rather drastic ways. When you leave for a vacation there is no need to attach a spook to your home that is guaranteed to turn out all the lights in Birmingham if someone should attempt to relieve you of your latest video equipment during your absence. But there are ways of preventing burglaries in the first place and deterring would-be thieves if you know how.

Purpose. These techniques can be used to protect property, people, pets or anything you like, or employed to ensure the safety of your possessions during any period of absence. I have used them constantly over many years, mainly for other people, with phenomenal results. On one occasion some friends of mine, who were planning a week or so away, asked for a protection to be placed round their home. I worked the Anubis ray and left it with that deity to care for the house in my friends' absence. All went well until they returned, when a next door neighbour, and one or two other people in the street, enquired of them as to why they had left a large black dog around the house in their absence and who had been responsible for feeding the beast. They protested that no such arrangement had been made and asked for a description of the animal. One person reported it as being 'a sort of Alsatian thing' while another described it as 'Egyptian looking, with big ears'. Needless to say it was never seen again, but it did the trick, thanks to Anubis.

Method 1. The spirits of the elements. This method is only for those experienced in magic who are used to working with these intelligences. *Salamanders* are first class protectors of the person but not always the best for protecting property, the reason being that, like certain guard dogs, rather than inhibit entry they tend to let the intruder in and then sort him out, in some cases with near fatal results. By all means ask your salamander to protect you personally, but do not leave him or his friends around your home when you are away. As the violators of King Tut's tomb discovered to their chagrin, the end results could be disastrous, unless the offender happens to be on good working terms with the little fiery chaps and able to counter-command your original instructions. Far better to request the aid of the elements of air or the elements of earth. The former (*sylphs*) will work as distractors, i.e., a burglar sees your property and his eyes gleam at the prospect of its contents. The instructed sylphs quickly catch on (they always do, their *forte* being mental activity and movement) and so commences the process of distraction. Doubts will begin to assail our criminal: perhaps there isn't anything in there worth having, after all; and what about the big house down the road, the people who own that are reputedly well-heeled, that might be a better bet; and so forth. Sylphs work via the mental processes. *Gnomes,* being the element of earth, work more practically, making entry difficult, doors impossible to break through, locks all securely fastened and a convenient bobby around at just the right moment. If, dear magician, you place an air or earth elemental on a property to protect it, for goodness' sake remember to dismiss it and thank it at the end of the run. Otherwise, your friends on their return may be sorely troubled, as no elemental likes being indefinitely trapped in a situation and will make its presence felt in no uncertain way if it feels it has been forgotten.

Method 2. The gods or archetypal forces. There are several god-forms or specialized rays that act as excellent protectors. Property and practical matters generally come under the jurisdiction of Horus and Hathor, but Nephthys can also play a useful role here. That which cannot be seen or of which one is not aware is unlikely to attract attention or merit attack, which consideration leads us straight to the domains of Nephthys, the hidden or invisible one.

The *Nephthian invocation* can be carried out ritually or mentally, but a degree of symbology of some measure should be employed. Nephthys's sigils being the cup or container and the lotus, and her element water, a suitably filled chalice or cup should be prepared. A representation of the place to be guarded should then be drawn up either symbolically or practically and projected into the chalice with an accompanying prayer to the goddess to render it invisible to all unfriendly eyes. Of course, this will not cause the material structure to disappear but simply help to ensure that the wrong folk fail to notice or become aware of it. It will skip their glance, as it were. As with the Neptunian influence in astrology the Nephthian ray can be nebulous and confusing, as it operates on the elimination of unwanted energies by diffusing them. Any felon out to seek a suitable property to 'do over' will fail to notice a Nephthian protected habitation, become distracted by something else, lose interest in the idea or feel a little under the weather that evening. The Nephthian ray can also be used for personal 'masking', which works on the same principle. One draws one's aura in so that one can enter a room without causing heads to turn, or pass through a dangerous area of town without attracting the attention of the rabble raisers.

The *Hathor invocation* involves our old friend, Hathor's famous mirror. The principle for protection in this instance is the utilization of the clear side of the mirror *faced outwards* from the property, so that anyone with evil intent experiences his own vibes reflected back at him in no uncertain way. Hathor in her protective aspect is Sekhmet; and Sekhmet, as the legends tell us, can be somewhat unpleasant when she is out on the rampage. This ray was frequently used in ancient Egypt, resulting in quite a few nasty accidents to intruders; not that the dear goddess herself pursued them, wearing her lioness mask, but simply because they received the full backlash of their own intentions multiplied to the sixth (the number sacred to Hathor) and that was a pretty powerful force.

A word of advice to would-be protectors: I mention this ray as it is a valid form of protection but it should be used with extreme care, always ensuring that your own intentions are honest and true. Otherwise the whole force unleashed could end up rebounding on you and Hathor, as Sekhmet, can have a nasty temper if provoked.

Horus is the god to whom houses and homes are sacred. He is the deity to invoke if you are looking for a new residence or seeking to dispose of your existing one. His main symbol is the eye, but he was frequently portrayed in hawk form and it is in the latter guise that he is best invoked to fly forth and seek out the right dwelling for you, the believer. Once secured, his eye will protect it for you; all you have to do is to place a photograph or picture of the house in the centre of a representation of the eye (see page 113 illustrations) or mentally visualize a giant eye covering the whole structure. Horus's weapon is the shaft of light, which will appear in some natural way should an intruder put in an appearance. Some people known to me used this method to protect their property and a strange thing happened. While they were away for a long weekend a house a few doors away caught fire. The police and fire brigade arrived and three men were noticed escaping across the roofs, highlighted against the blaze. They were duly apprehended and turned out to be a much sought after gang who had chosen that night to 'do over' all the empty houses in the road.

The *Anubis method*. A nice, homely form of protection, this. The old guard-dog idea usually works. Even those felons who keep a piece of poisoned meat or a cannister of something nasty but sniffable on hand would be sore pressed to foist their offerings on a spirit dog. Besides, Anubis is master of anaesthetics and therefore well able to deal with dirty deeds on dark nights. He alone of the gods was granted a safe right of way through the underworld so, for the man in the street who needs a bit of other worldly assistance, who better to call upon? No ritual is necessary, just a sincere request to Anubis and a word of thanks at the end. For – as sure as eggs are eggs – if Anubis guards you'll find things just as you left them, even if the neighbours complain about unfamiliar dark looking hounds wandering around unfed in the vicinity at night.

Dedicating Your Home
When you take on a new house or office you may feel inclined to invoke a tutelary deity so that the ray of your choice permeates the building, bringing prosperity and harmony to all. So far, so good. But do choose your rays to harmonize with those mostly associated with the place. A home where there are several small children would naturally benefit from the Isis ray. Intellectuals would be more at home with Thoth and artistic folk with Horus or Bast. Dedicated career ladies would benefit from a dose of Hathor while the DIY types, intent upon effecting their own improvements, would be only too glad to have Ptah around. On the other hand, the Nephthian ray is not the best for youngsters, or the Horus ray for teenagers, and those not completely in harmony with the animal kingdoms should avoid Bast at all costs. If, therefore, you feel you would like the gods to help you, decide carefully what form you wish their support to take and then make the appropriate supplication. A home or property protected in this way is a happy establishment and one that brings peace and good luck to those who frequent it. Mind you, you will need to use a little common sense and not invoke Osiris and then proceed to decorate the whole place in red.

Revelation

Nephthys, goddess of revelation, is usually happy to oblige with her gifts. But is it always right for us to know? A cautionary word is certainly in order here. Never invoke Nephthys to reveal anything unless you are *absolutely sure that you can cope with the answer*. I personally knew a man who besought the goddess to reveal to him a former life in detail. Thrice he made the request, twice she refused, but finally his wish was granted. The revelation was so horrendous that he was unable to live with it and took his own life. Nephthys is the goddess of hidden things and sometimes her lesson is that things are best left that way, that is until such times as we are spiritually adult enough to confront the outcome of our own past misdeeds or future trials. Nephthys is invoked through the chalice and the lotus. Both symbols can give peace and tranquillity to the supplicant, so why not simply invoke her in that context and thus come to terms with revelation within your own mind?

Academics

Many a poor student is unable to afford the books needed to cope with his or her chosen subject. Nobody is a better supplier of books than Thoth. A prayer to him, or an invocation for help to the keeper of the divine library, will produce the necessary volumes in a phenomenal way *unless you are on the wrong track*. During one period in my life when I was doing a lot of public speaking I would find that books appeared on my doorstep (someone dumped a pile of about sixteen one night and to this day I have never discovered who) and, although they often pertained to studies I was not necessarily involved in at that time, I could be certain that their subject matter would come up at my next talk; Thoth was helping me to prepare for it. If your thirst for knowledge is genuine, have no hesitation in asking the favour of this god. But, remember, as keeper of the Akashic records he knows more about you than you probably know yourself, so he will see in your mind whether your intentions are wise, foolish, egotistical or humble and dispense his favours accordingly.

There are many occasions when we don't get what we want in life, even if we beseech the gods for it on bended knees and with the full works. But it will not be the gods who deny us this; it will be ourselves who, by choice of our karma for this life, have decided that it is not for us. The body will protest, no doubt, the senses rebel and the sense of injustice rankle with us. Better, by far, to seek out what we are *really* here for and, having discovered our true karma, make out our requests to the gods for the strength to fulfil it. There will be no need to go without food to buy books, keep your family short in order to espouse some way-out religious mortification that denies you a living wage, or pursue some expensive gimmick in the name of progress at the expense of your health and sanity. It may not necessarily be easy, as the food of light is seldom served on a golden platter; but, with the aid of Thoth, you may gain a better insight into what is right for *you* at any given time during the course of this or any other of your many lives in the infinity of time.

Pyramid Initiation and Time Travel
An enthusiastic but inexperienced student of matters occult approached me, not so long ago, regarding a suitable technique for using pyramid power for self-development through the path of initiation. He had heard, apparently, that if he discovered the way the pyramid initiations took place he could skip happily through the experience and really get ahead in his occult development. Sorry, folks, my answer in this book must be the same one I gave to the young man in question: it simply can't be done. There are books available which give details of the original purpose for which the pyramids were built, as has been explained earlier in this work; anyone who has put in any study on the subject will know about the stone sarcophagus that originally stood at a given angle in relation to the Sun and fixed stars and in which the initiate was entombed for the required period. We are informed that the pyramids were not originally constructed as tombs, although they were frequently utilized for this purpose during dynastic times. Peter Lemesurier's detailed study, *The Great Pyramid Decoded* (Compton Russell Element), fills in all the details for those interested.

Pyramid initiation comes to one when the time is right and that is usually in the hands of Thoth. So I am afraid one cannot hammer on the initiatory door and expect it to open at one's command, and that's that. However, one can employ the pyramid principle in its time context for a little 'out of time' exploration. The technique is a simple one, but it can be dangerous unless one is well versed in the art of occult self protection. For those who feel they are advanced enough to risk it, the entry into the required mental state should be undertaken in the prone position and after sufficient meditation to produce a steady flow of the alpha brain pattern. It is not necessary to go on to theta waves; in fact, it can be a disadvantage. Once mentally and physically prepared, the visualization should be of a *crystal pyramid* in which one is encased and sealed. If you are doing it correctly a sense of timelessness or a suspension of the time factor will follow. From this point of timelessness the mind can be trained to home in on particular time zones, or points in the past history or future unfoldment of events here on Earth, or in any part of the universe in fact. The only limitation is the degree of mental/mystical expansion attained and the wisdom or soul age of the student. Time travel is not necessarily astral projection. It is the act of allowing that part of the soul or spirit that is in the timeless state to inject into the right hemisphere of the brain a series of impulses that are then relayed to the left hemisphere, at which point they are translated into pictures, shapes, emblems or words that are recognizable terms of reference here in the present. Learning to control this function is extremely difficult, interpreting the experiences is mind boggling and, assuming that you get somewhere with it, learning to live with its mind blowing relevations is an initiation in itself.

For Animals

Occultists are often asked by animal lovers if there are any magical formulae for protecting their pets and bringing them back if they are lost. Anubis is the great finder of lost things and this applies just as much to the animal kingdoms as to people or material objects or possessions. And, of course, he has a close affinity with the canine breed. But as representative of the animal kingdoms Bast is the Egyptian deity to invoke if your pet is lost, sick or giving you cause for concern. A collar or identification tag can be inscribed with a Bast or Anubis symbol, or even a simple request such as 'May Bast protect ...', or 'Anubis guard ...' if you prefer the canine vibes.

There are several effective visualization techniques for bringing home lost animals. The best known and simplest employs the symbol of the crescent moon holding the solar disk, the idea being to make a mental picture of the lost one and place the symbol over its head. Attach a golden thread to the animal in your mind's eye, allowing the light of the Sun/Moon to illuminate its path, and slowly draw it back to you. Sometimes animals leave their homes deliberately because they find it difficult to harmonize with the vibes of their owners. Cats, in particular, are prone to do this and it does not necessarily have anything to do with food. So maybe your pet has found itself a home more conducive to its own psychic frequency, bed and board alone not being sufficient to hold the animal kingdoms in situations where they do not feel spiritually at ease. A prayer or meditation to Bast will help to enlighten you on this point.

When your animal is approaching death, never be afraid to call on Bast or Anubis to help it through the transition. Animals do not view the act of dying in the same way that humans do. Of course they fear the method of death; who doesn't? And all too frequently they are subjected to a considerable amount of unnecessary suffering before the final release. But if allowed to pass naturally they are usually at peace.

18. GENERAL CORRESPONDENCES

Does the Egyptian god-system correspond to the archetypal forms depicted in the tarot or the planetary forces in astrology? This is a question that is bound to crop up. Let us start first of all with astrology. Since the original Egyptian deities were not primarily of this solar system we are left with a few large question marks here. The Greeks did a fair job of equating certain Egyptian gods with their own pantheon, but even they noticed the gaps. To allot planetary or zodiacal rulerships to the Egyptian divinities is no easy task for, to be truthful, they don't really fit; but obviously there are signs and planets that do harmonize with some of the Egyptian rays so, for those who like to plan their workings astrologically, I will make a brave attempt at some correspondences.

The Roman poet Gaius Manilius (first century B.C.) produced the following little rhyme when asked which gods ruled which signs:

Pallas rules the woolly Ram and Venus guards the Bull,
Apollo has the handsome Twins and Mercury the Crab.
Jove, with the Mother of the Gods, himself is Leo's lord.
The Virgin with her ear of corn to Ceres falls, the Scales
To Vulcan's smithy, while to Mars the warlike Scorpion cleaves.
The Hunter's human part Diana rules, but what's of horse
Is ruled by Vesta with the straitened stars of Capricorn.
Aquarius is Juno's sign as opposite to Jove,
And Neptune owns the pair of Fish that in the heavens move.

Relating this to the Greek pantheon we have: Pallas – Athene; Venus – Aphrodite; Mercury – Hermes; Jove – Zeus; Ceres – Demeter; Vulcan – Hephaestus; Mars – Ares; Diana – Artemis; Vesta – Hestia; Juno – Hera; and Neptune – Poseidon.

Herodotus, Plutarch and their contemporaries varied in their opinions as to how the Greek gods equated with their Egyptian predecessors, but some of the better known links were: Apollo – Horus; Hermes – Thoth; Hephaestus – Ptah; Aphrodite – Hathor (or Nephthys in some cases); Demeter – Isis; Artemis – Bast; Zeus – Amon; Hera – Mut. However, even in those days scholars disagreed among themselves, as it is firmly stated in some works that the Sun in Leo was worshipped as the god Osiris and the Sun in Virgo as Isis his wife, while Anubis and not Thoth ruled Cancer. Scorpio was also assigned to Set as the enemy of Horus. Another source gives the birthday of Horus as 24 July, making him a Leo, while the horse figure from the Egyptian mysteries ties him in with the Sagittarian principle. The connection between Thoth/Hermes and the zodiacal sign of Cancer is a puzzling one, although Mercury is sometimes named as ruler of Cancer's second decan. But then, as Dane Rudyhar so wisely observed, 'The measurements of astrology are symbolic and have to be translated into human qualities.'

From my own experience with the Egyptian archetypes I would say that the nearest planetary correspondences would be as follows, although even these leave room for doubt. But they are at least harmonious.

VENUS – Bast (or Hathor)
MERCURY – Thoth
JUPITER – Horus
SUN – Osiris (or Horus)
MOON – Isis
PLUTO – Anubis
SATURN – Ptah (or Thoth)
NEPTUNE – Nephthys
URANUS – Hathor (or Ptah)

This naturally brings the gods named into line with the associated zodiacal signs, although it will be noted that we do not have an Egyptian Mars. The scribes of old usually associated Set with the warrior ray and the sign of Scorpio, leaving Hathor in her Sekhmet role to take care of Aries.

The origin of the tarot is a subject always guaranteed to provoke a debate, but there is a strong school of thought that dates its symbology back to ancient Egyptian times, so in theory it should be easy to associate Egyptian god-forms with the Major Arcana. In spite of the numerological variations some obvious associations jump up and assail our visionary senses. No. 1, The Magician, for example, is obviously Thoth, and the role of No. 2, The High Priestess, fits Isis perfectly. Hathor takes good care of No. 3, The Empress, and Horus is No. 4, The Emperor. The Hierophantic role appears right for Osiris as the king/priest; Anubis is the foolish man who goes with a laugh where angels fear to tread; Bast is the gentle lady in No. 11, Strength, who opens the jaws of her leonine cousin as though they were the folds of a silken bag; and Nephthys, in her fusing rather than diffusing role, would be comfortably at home at No. 14, Temperance. Of course one could equally argue that No. 7, The Chariot, is worthy of Horus, while No. 19, The Sun, would suit Osiris. Bast and her kindred have much in common with the twin lion gods of Sirius at No. 17, The Star; the Last Judgment could fall to Thoth, Anubis or Osiris, all deities associated with the halls of judgment, or equally with No. 8, Justice. So there we are. There are no hard and fast rules just as long as the rays are harmonious and one avoids old 'Uncle Set' at No. 15.

Now let us take a quick glance at masonry which abounds with Egyptian symbology, as those versed in its chapters will well know. But once again we are faced with several masonic systems, none of them identical. English masons often claim that masonry was brought to these shores at the time of Athelstan and therefore predates the European medieval schools. We are informed that one Laurence Demott rose from Arch Mason to Grand Master of English masonry and produced the famous *Ahiman Rezon* or *Book of Constitutions* around the time of Mozart, the latter having highlighted the craft so vividly in his opera *The Magic Flute*. So whether, like some British masons, you claim your origins in the old Kilwinning Lodge or, as do many Europeans, you feel that your stuff goes right back to Egypt's earliest days, or even to Atlantis, there is still the connection with Egyptiana, if only in principle.

Mozart's *Die Zauberflöte (The Magic Flute)* is worthy of examination as it contains a wealth of Egyptian magical symbology in the masonic idiom. The archetypal correspondences are informative, and the evolutionary journey of the soul through the trials of earthly life to the halls of Isis and Osiris is brilliantly portrayed musically. Many people fail to connect Papageno, the bird catcher, with the cat family, a line borrowed from the Templars who held the Ptah/Bast/Imhotep triad in great reverence. The peal of bells used in the opera originated in the sistrum of Bast and, if the symbology is correctly adhered to, a sistrum should be employed in productions of this work. But few producers appear to be familiar with the depth of the subject, many treating it purely as a kind of fairytale pantomime, while those who have masonic connections themselves make a good job of disguising the secrets and not letting the proverbial cat out of the bag. A particularly fine example of occult music in *Die Zauberflöte* is the song of the armed men in the finale:

Der, welcher wandelt diese Strasse voll Beschwerden,
Wird rein durch Feuer, Wasser, Luft und Erden,
Wenn er des Todes Schrecken über winden kann,
Schwingt er sich aus der Erde himmel an.
Er leuchtet wird er dann im Stande sein,
Sich den Mysterien der Isis ganz zu weih'n.

Man, wandering on his road, must bear the tribulation
Of fire and water, earth and air's probation
If he prevails against the lures of evil's might
He soon will know the joys of Heaven's delight.
Enlightened, he will himself now prepare
The holy mysteries of Isis all to share.

Translation by Ruth and Thomas Martin.
G. Schirmer, New York/London.

The structure of this contrapuntal piece is more than merely masonic (with due apologies to all masons), for the Egyptian god (and I am convinced that there was one) who inspired Mozart on the day that he wrote it well understood the subtle effects of the musical intervals on the chakras. It is written in the classic masonic key of E flat, which is significant in itself and highly reminiscent of the *Terra Tremuit* from the Gregorian 'proper' of the old Tridentine mass for Easter Sunday. Mozart, however, refrains from some of the masonic knocks and sonorities employed by Beethoven (who was also a mason) in his

Missa Solemnis and keeps more to the old Egyptian theme, almost in defiance of the powerful Catholic influence of his day. One day we might be treated to a production of the opera that really caters for the old Egyptian magical themes upon which its Hermetic masonic descendant was originally based.

Books on divination were common in Egypt and many methods popular in our present day and age were in everyday use all those centuries ago. The Egyptians favoured scrying into clear water or crystals to aid their psychic faculty, or ESP, and the temple folk were dab hands at psychometry. Elements, trees and birds were considered omens or indications of the will of the gods and there were divining arrows made specially without points.

Mediumship of all kinds was also the thing in those ancient times, this taking the form of oracles which were communications from the gods to favoured persons. These were always delivered in a holy place, shrine or temple, and included prophetic powers, clairvoyance, second sight, or any other name you may choose for the faculty from the full range of semantics available in the literature of modern psychology. Even the early Christians, it would seem, were not averse to a little 'enquiry' and, among those who believed that the Egyptian mediums were on the mark, we can include such names as Tatian, Clement of Alexandria, Chrysostom, Origen, Justin Martyr, Cyprian, Tertullian, Jerome and Augustine. In fact, the latter referred thus to the prophetic powers of the spirits:

> They, for the most part, foretell what they are about to perform; for often they receive power to send diseases by vitiating the atmosphere. Sometimes they predict what they foresee by natural signs, which signs transcend human sense; at others they learn, by outward bodily tokens, human plans, even though unspoken, and thus foretell things to the astonishment of those ignorant of the existence of such plans.

The old chap was obviously highly in awe of the whole business, in spite of his Christian faith.

Healing was also practised in the old Egyptian temples and the methods employed were much the same as today. Mediums or psychics revealed the nature of the complaint and the sick person was put into 'magnetic' (hypnotic) sleep by those priests skilled in that craft. Isis was said to appear to them while they were 'under' to reveal the nature of their condition and why they were thus afflicted, which knowledge was supposed to render them whole upon waking. Shades of modern hypnotherapeutic techniques! There is nothing new under the Sun and most of the magical, mystical or psychical activities of the old Egyptian religion correspond to similar practices in modern occultism, religion and psychiatry.

Names and number we have already dealt with in an earlier chapter and, as there are several methods of numerology, it will again be up to the individual as to which he or she chooses to adopt. The Chaldean system of numbers differs from the Pythagorean, for example. Personally I find the simple 1 − 9 letters of the alphabet as good as any, but in the final analysis much will depend on the skill and personal inclination of the interpreter. A friend of mine, a reporter in the popular press, consulted four different numerologists; each had their own system and each gave her a different set of numbers; but the strange thing was that the end results were all the same, which goes to show that, no matter how much we cling to set tables of interpretation, in the final analysis it's all in the mind.

19. EGYPTIAN MAGIC AND TODAY'S RELIGIONS

It was Plato who remarked that magic consisted of the worship of the gods and Psellus who added that 'magic formed the last part of the sacerdotal science'. Does a belief in, or a subscription to, the efficacy of Egyptian magic therefore constitute the basis for a religion? And is organized religion right for the Aquarian Age? Questions, indeed, but answers can be attempted.

During his many years in psychiatric practice Jung noted an innate need in people for some form of acceptance of a higher principle. Whatever sort of banner you care to wave for that need, or whatever you choose to clothe it in, will be in accordance with your personal spiritual needs as a unique spark of the divine fire. For those who would like to choose the way of the Egyptian gods, or even their Atlantean or Siriun ancestors, there is a wealth of knowledge, comfort and warmth to be gained. Although on the surface it might appear that in this day and age anything goes, there are still bastions of Piscean orthodoxy raised firmly against the oncoming threshold of cosmic identity. But the Fishes must soon return to their watery home and Aquarius will bring in an age of individuality, where people will be free to express their religious leanings without fear of persecution or derision. As in the early days of any new-found freedom, the scales will no doubt occasionally swing too far in the opposite direction and out will go the baby with the bathwater. The Egyptians of old, or the Atlanteans who taught them, would have found it difficult to understand why, in order to grasp and blend with cosmic principles, some people today find it necessary to destroy the balance of their bodies with wrong food, drugs, violence, noise and inharmonious sounds calculated to cause a sure rift between the physical and etheric vehicles. Cosmic law and anarchism are opposites, as are love and chaos, one being the binding force and the other the rending force. It is perfectly possible to reach out into the spiritual cosmos and at the same time care for your neighbour, tend the sick, keep your body clean, be gentle, loving and yet firm in your own views.

The old Egyptian religion, in its purest form, is as valid today as it was centuries ago. The reason for this is that it was originally founded on true cosmic archetypes and *not* on the images and likenesses of men. Many people will scorn the idea of seeing God in anything other than human form; that is a normal development in the ego-tripping days of the young soul as it is associated with a sort of spiritual tribalism, the 'our sort are the best' syndrome. Many of the major religions dominant today fall into this category and these will be the prime movers against a resurgence of anything Egyptian. So, dear people, if you feel an affinity with the cosmic gods of old (and what is age in eternal timelessness?) it might be wise not to shout it from the mountain tops. Magical religions spread through spiritual attractions and not overt missionary work. You will not need to mount a soap box in Hyde Park to tell people about the joys to be gained through service to Bast, the strength and healing of Horus or the gentle wisdom of Isis. Simply get on with your own thing in true Aquarian fashion and soon the beacon of light that you have sparked will serve as a subtle attraction to others of like mind.

Magical religions are never easy to talk about, except to people of similar inclination, and the evangelical approach simply doesn't go with a cosmically orientated discipline that is not bounded by dogma or set creed.

Many readers will not fail to observe, however, certain similarities between popular contemporary religious practices and beliefs and the ancient religion of Egypt. Horus, for example, was born of a virgin, his father already having ascended into Heaven and his mother being made pregnant by the magical power of a bird-headed god. Perhaps Thoth isn't referred to in 'holy spirit' terms, but the principle of a higher intervention is the same. Saviour gods, like Horus, inevitably appear in the same guise in all beliefs. Their birth is traditionally phenomenal, with an intervening force taking a hand while their true father resides aloft in some unapproachable, celestial sphere. They are depicted as comely, wise and gentle, with the love theme frequently featured as the central pivot of their message.

Many Christian festivals had their origins in Egypt of old. The 21 December, being the shortest day, suggested to the Egyptians Osiris's entombment in the tamarisk tree from which he was miraculously rescued on the third day, giving them cause for rejoicing on 25 December. But, then, many of the saviour gods were associated with death or suffering in or on a sacred tree. Odin was painfully suspended from the Yggdrasil until, after three days, he noticed the runes at his feet and painfully stretched himself forth to grasp them. Whereupon, he was immediately relieved of his suffering and granted the gift of true knowledge. Osiris was similarly blessed after his resurrection. Runic magic and Egyptian magic are very compatible.

An examination of the ancient Egyptian texts throws a very different light on certain fundamentalist interpretations of the Christian Bible. The scriptures cannot be taken too literally in the light of the history, religious beliefs and cultures prominent in the civilized world during the period when they were supposed to have taken place. There are several excellent books available on this subject for those with open minds and a thirst for the truth, and the historical aspects of the scriptures have received a considerable amount of coverage on the more educational-type television channels over the past few years. Of course, diehards will argue that the biblical offerings were divinely inspired, but what's sauce for the goose also goes well with the gander. For the believer in the Egyptian religion, Thoth has been just as busy hovering over his scribes down the ages as his feathered biblical contemporary.

The Egyptian system can form a sound religious basis for those who would like to treat it in that light. While not appearing in as barbaric a mode as certain later pantheons the Egyptian god-forms are tinged with a warm understanding of human frailties; they also display spiritual qualities that manifest as an earnest desire to help all living creatures to negotiate safely the rock-strewn paths of their earthly karma. Many people I have known personally have derived great comfort, love and enlightenment from the Egyptian way so, if you feel you have a strange leaning towards the old gods but have suffered the doctrinal programming of modern credos, why not become a 'born again follower of Isis'? As Bishop Cecil Northcott remarked when reviewing the book *Isis in the Graeco-Roman World* in a popular daily a year or so ago, 'In a day when the cults are on the way up and the most weird beliefs pass as religion, a few doses of Isis might be worth having.'

20. SIRIUS – THE NEW COSMIC MAGIC

The star Sirius has obviously held considerable significance for mankind since the earliest recorded times. However, the Egyptians were not the only ancient race to accord special powers to this stellar beacon. Dogon records telling its story go back to antiquity, as we have already noted, and the dog-star has enjoyed many names and titles throughout the magical and religious history of our planet.

Let us take a brief astronomical look at this luminary. Sirius is a white star in the constellation of Canis Major, some eight and a half light years away from Earth. It is the brightest star in the heavens, unless we are to accept a more recent discovery in the Tarantula Nebula. For the time being, however, we will give our enigmatic stellar friend the benefit of the doubt.

Around the middle of the last century the astronomer Bessel studied Sirius over a period of time; he noted a perturbation in its movement indicative of the presence of another body within a proximity proportionally close enough to effect a gravitational pull of some considerable force. Yet his research revealed no trace of a mass large enough to affect a star the size of Sirius. Some years later a very small body was observed orbiting Sirius and its orbital period was calculated to be about fifty years. This second star became known as Sirius B, sometimes called Digitaria. Recently astronomers have learned more about the nature of 'white dwarfs', that is stars that don't give out much light but exert an enormous gravitational pull because of their atomic structure. A white dwarf is a star that has 'collapsed', which means that the atoms have become so densely packed that the nature of its substance hardly equates at all to matter as we know it. When atoms are compressed to such an extent the resulting mass becomes so heavy that, to give an example, a cubic foot of the matter of Sirius B would weigh 2,000 tons and a match box full of the star's core would weigh approximately 50 tons.

Some astronomers believe they have seen a third star in the Sirius system. A man named Fox claimed to have seen it in 1920; and in 1926, 1928 and 1929 it was supposedly seen by van den Bos, Finsen and others at the Union Observatory. Then suddenly it seemed to make itself invisible. More recently Irving W. Lindenblad of the U.S. Naval Observatory in Washington, D.C., probed the Sirius system, but failed to detect a third star although he gleaned much additional information about Sirius B in the process.

The Dogons considered Sirius B to be far more important than its larger and brighter companion. They also possessed knowledge of the third luminary as well as a small planet in the system and there is some confusion as to whether the third star was believed to be a smaller sun or simply a large planet, since this ancient African tribe also made reference to the 'shoe-maker's planet' and a 'planet of women'.

Sirius's association with the Egyptian system is primarily through the very earliest sources that connect Egyptian beliefs with a race of colonizers, whose origins are historically obscure but around whom a whole mythology has evolved. Call these people ancient astronauts, Atlanteans or anything you like – it matters not – but somehow their magical system has filtered down through the ages. Many reliable psychics and mystics firmly subscribe to the idea of a special gene, or personalized 'time capsule', programmed with the knowledge of the 'old ones' who came from the Sirius system centuries ago; this gene has been passed down from generation to generation to the present day. From this Siriun genetic strain a new school of magic has emerged. It could be called 'mind magic' or 'thought magic', as it operates purely on a mental level and does not rely upon any form of practical ritual or ceremony. Material offerings, spoken prayers and the like are unnecessary in its practice; all is passed from mind to mind.

Since Siriun magic shares its archetypes with some of the very earliest Egyptian magical references, there are some symbols that are equally valid in both systems. The eye, itself forming part of the hieroglyph for the name of Osiris, and the star are two examples. The sacred Siriun numbers are five and eight and, like the cloak of Isis, the colour associated with the larger star is blue. The smaller star responds to the Osiris colours of white or green. The two colours (blue and green) create that turquoise hue so evident in all early Egyptian art. The uraeus also has Siriun connotations, as does the lion, although the cat family as a whole is deeply bound up with Siriun evolutionary development and cosmic identity. Thus we have the association with No. 11 in the tarot Major Arcana, *Strength,* which portrays a gentle woman calmly opening the jaws of a full grown lion.

What, then, is this 'thought magic'? How does it work and where does Sirius fit in? Thought or mind occultism will be the new magic of the Aquarian Age as it is truly cosmic in nature. It observes the rules of cosmic law in that it fully acknowledges all correspondences without requiring outward manifestations of their principles, the inner state of mind being more important. Since telepathy plays a major role within this system, it presents a doorway to a future age where each individual will have his or her own line of communication with the archetypal forces without the need for intermediaries. There are whole areas of mind magic that are, as yet, untapped. In future generations man will learn to develop and use these to create a whole new technology, but at present their manifestation is limited to the metaphysical field.

Of course, we are looking a long way ahead, but the ball has to start rolling at some point. The world may not be ready to stop strap-hanging on leatherbound dogmas, or to shirk its individual responsibilities by placing them on the scapegoat of some sacrificial redeemer who guarantees to do all the dirty work for them. But time can work wonders.

Siriun magic involves a conscious control of the left and right brain hemispheres, thus allowing the rational-thinking left side free access to the abstract, which can then be translated into terms sufficiently lucid to make sense both esoterically and exoterically. I have given a few examples already of how Egyptian magic can successfully employ mind-control techniques: the scales of Maat, for instance, where the principle is visualized. How many of us who practise these arts have our impedimenta at the ready when some drastic emergency occurs?

Some years ago, while travelling home by train rather late at night after giving a talk, I was assaulted by a highly inebriated and very violent 'gentleman'. In my mind I shouted to my friendly salamander for help. There was not a second's delay between my mental SOS and the little fire elemental's response. My attacker leapt back as though struck by an unseen force and started to tear at his collar, screaming that he was on fire. Sweat poured from his brow. He fell upon the floor and rolled about in considerable discomfort for a minute or so until we reached the next station, at which point he stumbled out, shouting for water.

I know better now how to control the measures I would employ in the defence of my person but, when one is starting out on the path and just becoming familiar with other intelligences of different power proportions, one tends, in one's lack of wisdom, to use sledge hammers to crack nuts.

But let us return to Sirius. The aspirant to the Sirius path must first learn to use his or her natural telepathic skills and develop these to a high degree. With the mind unfettered by earthly dimensions it is possible to reach out into the universe and make telepathic contact with many other life forms. If one has Siriun connections anyway, and I have personally encountered many people in the 'field' who do, then surely the most natural thing in the universe would be to pursue (or resume) mental correspondence with one's own cosmic roots.

So what sort of role does the Sirius ray play in our world? According to old teachings and traditions our solar system was seeded from Sirius, which means that cosmic impulses must have gone out from that direction in the infancy of our Sun. Hence the old Egyptian legends related earlier in this book. If we are to believe the axiom 'as above, so below' it is logical to assume that following those early impulses, which would have been purely of a mental or thought nature, later physical manifestations must have occurred to reinforce the original emphasis, i.e., the 'gods'. In a monotheistically-orientated society any suggestion of polytheism, or even the multiple nature of a single divinity, is viewed with suspicion (the Christian 'trinity' being the exception). However, once free of the limiting environmental programming of earthly dogmas, the nature and function of the evolving soul in an infinite and timeless universe and its role in the higher spheres becomes far clearer. The shattered hologram demonstrates how the tiny fragments of a broken picture can each contain the exact scene or pattern that was portrayed in the original whole. Why, then, cannot an infinite mind cast facets of itself in many directions, each of which is endowed with the complete nature of the whole? And, if beings that have developed and evolved in other parts of the universe accept their gods in different forms, by what right does dear old Earth send out the inquisitors? How boringly tribal and egotistical.

Having accepted a degree of responsibility for the raising and educating of this little old solar system, it seems logical to assume that the Siriun tutelaries would lurk about for a while to keep an eye on their wayward flock. The fact that during certain periods of Earth's history it is culturally or politically unfashionable to accept the existence of such beings, let alone pay fealty to them, does not cause them either to cease to exist or to remove their bountiful presences from our vicinity in disgust. If we are wise and caring parents we do not disown our children simply because they are passing through a period of development during which they reject our help and advice.

Sirius, as a star system, has a specific function that is related to what are popularly referred to in current esoteric parlance as 'evolutionary quantum jumps'. In other words, it acts as a sort of spiritual cosmic springboard from which the evolving soul, having arrived at a certain cosmic age, can gather together its energies and make ready to step into the next stage in its evolutionary development.

This naturally ties its influence in with such issues as 'missing links', particularly in relation to the utilization of somatically evolving strains as suitable vehicles for those souls who are ready to take on the task of adding a new dimension of intelligence to primitive beings. Nor is Sirius alone in its performance of this function in the hierarchical scheme of things, as it would appear that other stars of this nature act as transmuting agents for other planetary systems within a given radius.

Now, having established the role of Sirius as related to this planet, what about the magical system that accompanies this knowledge? Magic, in its positive application, is concerned with manipulating cosmic forces and learning to become the master of one's own environment. This covers a very wide field, from weather to personal psychology, and may not come within the spiritual terms of reference of everyone incarnate here.

Since Sirius is a binary system, deeply involved with the nature and psychology of 'twins', the law of polarity is of the utmost importance. The Sirius ray can bring twin souls together and strongly accent the need for a full and satisfying polarity. According to several authorities the larger and brighter of the two Sirius suns represented Isis, while the smaller dwarf star, known to ancient peoples as the 'eye star', was Osiris, the two forming one of the earliest recorded sets of divine twins. Occultly speaking, the larger of the two stars acts as a window to the universe through which the student soul can gaze in wonderment at the vastness of time and space, while the smaller star represents the more personal lessons to be learned by the individual.

Let us take healing as an example. Healing that involves the Sirius ray is best carried out by pairs of healers at the present stage of our Earth's development, but eventually the programme must become a self-healing one. Of course, there are a few advanced souls who are able to cope with a self-healing ray today. Some of them will also find it fairly easy to control their environment to a degree by employing the same mind power techniques.

The occult disciplines here on Earth are many and recent years have seen a revival of most of them in one form or another. They are, however, mainly of the nature of this planet itself and therefore totally parochial, except the Egyptian system which acts as a gateway to both the old Atlantean magic and its Siriun predecessor.

Adepts in certain occult paths may strongly disagree with my last statement and argue that their discipline fully accommodates all abstract states. That is their prerogative. The Siriun ray, however, aims to bring the knowledge from the finer levels of consciousness into fundamental practicality, so that its fruits become manifest in such avenues as scientific advancement, healing, medical help and general aids to an overall spiritual enlightenment that are not limited to an occult *élite*. Only by broadening its cosmic horizons will our planet, as a whole, step forward once more in its evolution, and those souls who feel that they are not yet prepared to negotiate such a move will be free to move to another part of the universe which is more congenial to their beliefs and outlook. Parallel universes do exist where every permutation of experience, both human and otherwise, is to be found.

These are but a few of the lessons to be learned through the magic of Sirius. It is possible, by rising above the immediate sphere of terrestrial activities, to avoid many of the turmoils generated by earthly evils and also stay well clear of those magical practitioners of malign intent who limit their spheres of activity to the immediate environment of this planet.

Of course, it would be occultly illogical to assume that Earth is the only place in the cosmos where one is likely to come up against evil, or misplaced energy. Such states are to be encountered anywhere in the universe. But, when functioning purely in the mind-state, one also learns the correct mental techniques for combating it. In other words, the capacity for defence expands with the growth and development of outward spiritual seeking, in accordance with the occult law of equalities. So the whole process does, in fact, have the effect of making it easier to cope with the stresses and strains of mundane earthly existence, if only in showing the spirit what a very small part of the universal jigsaw is the passing worry and how quickly the passage of time will eradicate the tension and come up with a new crossword puzzle to be solved by the clues provided by evolutionary experience.

I am frequently asked to recommend textbooks on this or that occult system. No simple matter; in spite of the wealth of literature available on magic generally, there is little of practical value covering the Egyptian discipline and, anyway, no matter how much one reads, when it comes to the nitty-gritty, there will always be a situation arising that is not covered anywhere in written instructions. I didn't learn magic from textbooks myself, but later discovered that most of the conclusions experience had taught me accorded with the signposts encountered by earlier travellers along the same road.

Therefore, with regard to learning Siriun magic, there are no books that I can, in good conscience, recommend on the subject. I can only comment that the Egyptian system offers the best 'open sesame' to the Sothian *sanctum sanctorum*. A fair knowledge of the Hermetic disciplines, correspondences and philosophy and a strict observance of the law of polarity is essential. Positive and negative should be fully understood in their esoteric sense and not purely related to states of good and evil or to physical sexual characteristics. I once heard the following description, which is apt and succinct:

'The positive/occultist/magician is the person who is gifted in the manipulation of cosmic forces, while the negative/receptive/sensitive/medium is the person whose talents enable him or her to be manipulated by cosmic forces.'

Full and detailed descriptions of the subtle differences between these two states, plus the role of the mystic, are given in *Practical Techniques of Psychic Self-Defence*. There are, of course, certain people whose angle of polarity takes them very near to the 'centre'. In other words, they can perform as either a medium or magus, but this usually only occurs in older souls or those who have completed a twinning.

When working in mind magic mental discipline is a *must*. Never should the mind be allowed to wander off unreined. Being human, none of us find this easy, so perfection in the technique can only be aimed for. The mind that cannot quickly compute surprise situations and re-programme normal emotional responses to such stimuli will suffer as a result, often with psychosomatic repercussions.

But the other edge of the sword offers the venturesome psyche the power to achieve all the necessary adjustments, as the forces both for and against the soul's advancement via the channels of mind magic are equally balanced. For example, the student of the Siriun system may receive some pretty mind-blowing shocks from time to time, but the system also gives him or her the mental resilience and necessary occult know-how to cope with them, to heal any rifts and to re-balance the ego.

The nature of pure energy is brought to the fore in mind magic, part of the discipline being the ability to draw cosmic energy at will and channel it according to the levels at which it is required. One constantly hears talk of systems that deal only with either spiritual matters or more practical considerations. In the Siriun school, however, all energy is from the same source, so it can be fashioned into deeper spiritual comprehensions on the one hand or more material needs on the other. However, the ethics in any magical operation, as well as the magic itself, must rest with the individual. If the energies drawn are over-used at one particular frequency an imbalance will be caused that can have serious repercussions, usually at the level at which it has been abused. So, if you have a mind to use the system for financial gain, for example, watch that the overspill doesn't bring down your health. Siriun energies are self-monitoring in that they balance themselves evenly, regardless of how they are drawn upon, so this is certainly *not* the system for the 'know-all' or the hedonist.

The Siriun ray, from an astrological standpoint, is usually described as a mixture of Jupiter and Mars and any excess of expansive energies of this nature that are not properly handled can be as deadly as an overdose of radiation. Equally, if you have it in mind to spend your time staying out of your body for long periods surveying the universe or travelling backward or forward in time (the Siriun ray being very much bound up with the nature of time), there might well come the day when you experience difficulty in returning and assuming full physical control. This could result in a breakdown of the nervous system or one of the many other manifestations of the schizophrenia syndrome. Hence the absolute necessity for balance between the spiritual and material worlds and for emotional stability and a good polarization. Poking around other time zones to see what your related soul fragments are up to may be very fascinating, but the fragment that is here, in this present time zone, has a task to complete and needs to stay in control at this earthly point if it is to complement the whole and fulfil its karma.

If you feel drawn to Sirius and would like to sample its wares, work first through Egyptian magic in its earliest and purest form. The day will come when you will see a glimmer ahead in the tunnel of uncertainty. Slowly that pinprick will grow into a door through which the light of Sirius will shine in all its brilliance. Then you can take it from there.

CONCLUSIONS

The study of Egyptian magic is a deep and extensive one if followed through to its true conclusions; and yet it is not necessary to tackle it in such academic depths in order to avail oneself of its bounties. In ancient times the simple worker in the fields could call upon the power of the 'gods' (personalized aspects of the one god-source, or centre point, if you care to put it that way). All one needs, basically, is a little knowledge as to who takes care of what and how to go about approaching it or them. There are no hard and fast rules of application; the only *must* is a good mental discipline and rigid adherence to cosmic laws.

Needless to say, there will be some metaphysical legal-eagle who will ask for a definition of cosmic law, or a set of rules in triplicate from which he can quote the dos and don'ts. Cosmic laws are not earthly laws. They are concerned with the natural forces that hold the universe in equipoise. Cosmic concepts of right and wrong are all about order versus chaos; harmony versus disharmony; construction versus destruction; selflessness versus selfishness; and love versus hate. In other words, it's all in the mind of the individual and a question of the personalized conscience. This, in turn, will depend very much on the stage of spiritual development through which the psyche is passing in this particular zone of Earth time.

The directional impulses of cosmic law move in an orderly and forward motion. Sometimes pockets of energy turn tail and face the oncoming flow, as though in rebellion against it. This causes pain and suffering both to the wayward force itself and all those intelligences that go to make it up and, also, to those parts of the river of cosmic consciouness which it hits against in its upstream fight. These areas of conflict occur throughout the universe in differing modes and intensities, but time finally pacifies them and they are once again swept forward to continue their cosmic journey of return to their creator. These head-on conflicts are what evil is all about – misplaced energy – which can manifest in any condition from the squalor of material poverty to the suffering of the soul that is lost 'out of time'. To the Egyptians evil was the serpent Apep, or Set, brother of Isis and Osiris. Set represented the anti-ray to light and love and his existence was wisely acknowledged.

In this time zone in which we now exist there is evil, and burying one's head in the sand and making a lot of sweet spiritual noises is not going to alter the fact. Better by far to know one's enemy and take a few precautions against bumping into him on a dark night in the marshes. These evil forces, or misplaced cosmic energies, can be called upon by people of unscrupulous intent but, as they are travelling in the opposite direction to the cosmic flow, they cannot draw their sustenance from the source of light which is the Creator. They therefore need to feed upon the energies of those who like to have them around. Hence the old legend that he who seeks the aid of Set must pay the price with his immortal soul or part with his *ka* or *ba*.

Like attracts like: a simple cosmic law that is easy to understand. So, if you want to work white magic, be sure that you yourself are clean in body, mind and spirit, or during your invocations you might end up with the minions of Set on your doorstep or Apep curled around your bedpost. Keeping on the right side of cosmic law means ensuring that your magical intentions are orderly, harmonious, constructive, selfless and loving. Generate all those feelings with true sincerity and it will be Isis who tucks you in and Bast who protects you from Apep. The Egyptian god-forms, or 'divine aspects', are very loving; anyone who claims they are not is either sending out the wrong signals themselves and getting back a dose of Hathor's mirror, or so unskilled in what they are doing as to be invoking the wrong thing in the first place. A tiny thread of disharmony can interrupt a genuine connection with a principle of light so, when there are several people working together, although most of them may be correctly spiritually orientated, the one who is not can press the red destruct button.

Egyptian magic can be approached in three ways. Intellectually, though a profound study of its philosophy, history, art, literature and traditions; through practical application; or a combination of both. It is not a static system, however, and will slowly lead the neophyte into deeper waters from which he can either retreat if he is unready, or proceed if he is of the right spiritual maturity. Never be ashamed to admit that you found it necessary to leave it all alone. It takes a wise man to be humble and so often one hears failure blamed on some unfortunate lodge master or group leader. All failure lies within ourselves. Whether or not we can handle this or that occult ray is not up to our teacher, the writer of this or that book, or those on the 'other side' whom we feel have failed to come up with the right answers when we needed them. The fact that you are the one who has dropped out while the others soldier on is indicative in itself that it has been you and not they who have chosen to stop at a given point. Now there's nothing wrong in that, as long as you don't start throwing stones at the train because you chose to alight at the earlier stop.

There will doubtless be many who will not find the Egyptian system suitable to their spiritual or occult needs. Fair enough. Then make it in your own way and in your own time. But, for those who do feel drawn to the ancient Egyptian, Atlantean or cosmic magic, I hope this book will ring many bells, open many doors and fire many torches to help you along the universal road that leads to the central source of all light and love.

APPENDIX

The following tables of dates are as given by Cyril Aldred in his book *The Egyptians* (Thames & Hudson) with some additional pieces of information.

Early Prehistoric Period

Date B.C.	Northern or Lower Egypt	Southern or Upper Egypt	Main Sites	Period
c.5000	Faiyum 'A'		Faiyum depression	
		Tasian	Deir Tasa, Mosta-gedda	Neolithic
c.4000		Badarian	el-Badari	Chalcolithic
	Merimda		Merimda	
		Amratian	el-Amra, Nagada, el-Ballas, Hu, Abydos, Mahasna	Early Pre-dynastic
c.3600				

Later Prehistoric Period

Date B.C.	Northern or Lower Egypt	Southern or Upper Egypt	Main Sites	Period
c.3600		Early Gerzean		Middle and Late Pre-dynastic
	Maadi		el-Maadi	
c.3400		Late Gerzean	el-Gerza, Haraga	
c.3200	The union of Upper and Lower Egypt under one king		Hierakonpolis Memphis Abydos	Historic

Archaic Period (Dynasties I and II)

Approx Date B.C.	Principal Kings	Funerary Customs	Significant Events
3200	**Dynasty I**		Development of writing, copper tools and weapons
	Menes (Narmer)	Royal burials in main tomb at Saqqara	
	Ity I (Hor-Aha)		Trade with Levant
	Ity II (Djer)		
	Merbiapen (Adjib)	Cenotaphs at Abydos	Expeditions to Sudan
2900	**Dynasty II**		
	Hetep-sekhem-wy	Private burials near tomb or cenotaph of the king	Use of stone in building and for statuary
	Neb-re		
	Ni-neter		
	Peribsen		Religious and political strife
	Kha-sekhem-wy		Pacification of the Two Lands
2660			

Old Kingdom (Dynasties III and IV)

Date B.C. and Years of Reign	Principal Kings	Main Sites	Funerary Customs	Significant Events
c.2660	**Dynasty III**			
	Sa-nakht		Royal burial in Step Pyramid	Large-scale building and sculpture in stone
19	Neter-khet (Djoser)	Saqqara		
			Private mastabas near Royal tomb	
6	Sekhem-khet	Sinai	(Hesi-re, Methen)	
24	Huny			
c.2600	**Dynasty IV**			
			Evolution of true pyramid and climax	Great technical & artistic mastery
24	Sneferu	Maidum	of its development.	over most materials.
23	Khufu (Kheops)	Dashur	Private burial in	The classic age of
31	Khafra (Khephren)	Giza	mastabas and some	the Old Kingdom
18	Menkaure (Mykerinus)	Bubastis	rock-tombs	
c.2500				

Later Old Kingdom (Dynasties V and VI)

Date B.C. and Years of Reign	Principal Kings	Main Sites	Funerary Customs	Significant Events
c.2500	**Dynasty V**			Rise in importance of
8	Weser-kaf		Royal pyramids smaller, but	Heliopolis
15	Sahu-re	Saqqara	adjuncts decor-	
11	Ne-weser-re	Abusir	ated with fine	Expeditions
28	Djed-ka-re Isesi	Heliopolis	reliefs	to Punt.
30	Wenis		*Pyramid Texts*	Private sculpture in wood
			Gradual increase in size of private mastabas	and stone of high standard
c.2340	**Dynasty VI**		(Ti, Mereruka)	
15	Teti	Deir- el-Gebrawi		Decentralization of government
44	Pepy I (Phiops I)	Koptos	Rock-tombs in	
5	Mer-en-re I	Abydos	provincial centres	Rise in feudalism,
90	Pepy II (Phiops II)	Saqqara		leading to anarchy
c.2180				

Middle Kingdom (Dynasties XI to XIII)

Date B.C. and Years of Reign		Principal Kings	Main Sites	Funerary Customs	Significant Events
c.2080		**Dynasty XI**		*Coffin Texts*	
	51	Menthu-hotep I Neb-hepet-re	Thebes	Large rock-tomb with pyramid in forecourt	Reunion of Two Lands
	12	Menthu-hotep II S-ankh-ka-re	Abydos		
c.1990		**Dynasty XII**			Development of Literature
	30	Amun-em-het I (Ammenemes)	Thebes	Royal burials in pyramids	
	44	Sen-wosret I (Sesostris)	Lisht	Private burials in mastabas and rock-tombs	Large irrigation schemes in Faiyum. Re-building on all sites. Final suppression of feudal nobles
	18	Sen-wosret II	Dahshur		
	36	Sen-wosret III	Lahun		
	50	Amun-em-het III	Hawara		
c.1785		**Dynasty XIII**		Appearance of anthropoid coffin and shawabti-figure	Rise of Osiris-cult at Abydos. Subjugation of Nubia. Trade through Byblos with Syria and Aegean. Arrival of the Hyksos
		A large number of kings. Probably a separate line of rulers in Western Delta forming Dynasty XIV			
c.1640		**Dynasty XV/XVI**		There is little information available on this period	
c.1650		**Dynasty XVII**			Hyksos driven out

New Kingdom (Dynasties XVIII to XX)

Date B.C. and Years of Reign	Principal Rulers	Funerary Customs	Foreign Affairs	Significant Events
1570	**Dynasty XVIII**		Nubia and Kush under Egyptian Viceroy	Introduction of bronze and new weapons, horse and chariot
25	Ahmosis			
21	Amun-hotep (Amenophis I)		New dependencies in Palestine & Syria	
19	Tuthmosis I	Kings buried in elaborate rock-tombs at Thebes: separate mortuary temples	Diplomatic relations with	Glass-working
21	Q. Hatshepsut			
54	Tuthmosis III		Cyprus, Aegean,	Trade with
25	Amenophis II		Anatolia, Babylon	Punt restored
14	Tuthmosis IV			
			Fall of Knossos	
39	Amenophis III	Private burials in rock-tombs at Thebes & elsewhere gradually become less opulent: tendency for self-contained burial in highly decorated coffin. Magic funerary texts written on papyrus rolls *(The Book of the Dead)*	Loss of influence in Asia	Akhenaten's failure to impose monotheism
17	Amenophis IV (Akhenaten)			
9	Tut-ankh-amun		Rise of Hittites	
?	Haremhab			
				Appearance of iron weapons
1304	**Dynasty XIX**		Attempt to challenge	
13	Sethos I		Hittites in	Capital moved
67	Ramesses II		Syria. Treaty between Egypt and Hittites	from Thebes to Pi-Ramesse. Exodus of
12	Merenptah			Hebrews. Great
			Fall of Troy	building activity
1181	**Dynasty XX**		Ethnic movements in Mediterranean	
2	Set-nakht			
32	Ramesses III and eight other Ramessides		Eclipse of Hittites	Army recruits mercenaries
			Repulse of Libyans and Sea-Peoples	Decline in prestige of kingship
				Tomb robberies at Thebes
			Loss of Asiatic dependencies	Rebellion in Middle Egypt
1075				

Late Period (Dynasties XXI to XXXI)

Date B.C. and Years of Reign		Principal Kings	Chief Centres	Foreign Affairs	Significant Events
1075		**Dynasty XXI**		Dorian invasions of Greece. Growth of Phoenicia	Leadership of Delta
	45	Psusennes I	Tanis		
			Thebes		Libyan mercenaries
				Rise of Israel	achieve supremacy
940		**Dynasties XXII-XXIII**			Kush independent
	21	Sesonchis I	Bubastis	Sack of Temple at Jerusalem	
	36	Osorkon	Tanis		Skill in metal- and faience-work
	54	Pedubast	Thebes		Rising anarchy in Egypt provokes intervention of Kush
			Herakleopolis		
830		**Dynasty XXIV**		Revival of Assyrian power under Tiglath-Pileser III	
	5	Bocchoris	Sais		Amun-cult domin-ant at Napata and Thebes. Rebuild-ing at Thebes and elsewhere
751		**Dynasty XXV**			
	35	Pi-ankhy	Napata (Sudan)		
	15	Shabako	Thebes	Invasions of Egypt by Assyrians	
	20	Shebitku			Antiquarian study
				Sack of Thebes	of the past
	26	Taharqa			
664		**Dynasty XXVI**		Expulsion of Kushites	Revival in arts and crafts
	54	Psammetichos I	Sais		
				Independence from Assyrians achieved	Eclipse of Amun
	15	Necho II	Edfu		Philhellenism
	6	Psammetichos II	Saqqara	Excursion into Phoenicia. Trade with Greece. Anti-Persian intrigues	Greek mercenaries in pay of kings
	19	Apries (Hophra)	Daphnae		
	44	Amasis	Naukratis		
525-404		**Dynasty XXVII (Persians)**		Conquest of Egypt by Cambyses	
404-398		**Dynasty XXVIII**			Resistance to Persians weakened by dynastic squabbles
	7	Amyrteos	Sais	Eventual liberation with Greek aid	
398-378		**Dynasty XXIX**			
	13	Achoris	Mendes	Alliances against Persia	Last flourish of native arts
378-341		**Dynasty XXX**	Sebennytos		
	19	Nectanebo I	Bubastis	Repulse of Persian invasion (Pharna-barzus) 373 B.C.	The last native Pharaoh
	19	Nectanebo II	Edfu		
341-333		**Dynasty XXXI (Persians)**		Reconquest of Egypt by Persians	
332		Alexander of Macedon conquers Persian Empire			
332-304		Alexander the Great The Ptolemies – Cleopatra etc.			Egypt Hellenised

BIBLIOGRAPHY

The Occult Sciences	Arthur Edward Waite	(Kegan Paul, Trench, Trubner & Co. Ltd., 1981)
Cult of the Cat	Patricia Dale-Green	(Heinemann, 1963)
Egyptian Belief and Modern Thought	James Bonwick	(The Falcon's Wing Press, 1956)
The Egyptians	Cyril Aldred	(Thames & Hudson, 1961)
The Book of the Dead Volumes 1, 2 & 3 (From *Books on Egypt and Chaldea*)	A.E. Wallis Budge	(Kegan Paul, 1901 edition)
The Egyptian Mysteries	Iamblichos	(Wm. Rider & Son, 1911)
Thrice Greatest Hermes Volumes 1, 2 & 3	G.R.S. Mead	(Theosophical Publishing Co., 1906)
Larousse Encyclopedia of Mythology		(Paul Hamlyn)

Isis in the Graeco-Roman World	Dr. R.E. Witt	(Thames & Hudson, 1971)
A Dictionary of Symbols	C.E. Cirlot	(Routledge & Kegan Paul, 1962)
The Sirius Mystery	Robert K.G. Temple	(Sidgwick & Jackson, 1976)
The Magic Flute	W.A. Mozart, words by Ludwig Giesecke and Emanuel Schikenader. English translation by Ruth and Thomas Martin	(G. Schirmer, Inc. New York/ London)
The Great Pyramid Decoded	Peter Lemesurier	(Compton Russell Element)

Further Information

CARTOUCHE, an Oracle of Ancient Egyptian Magic, devised by Murry Hope, is now available from:

Thorsons Publishers Limited
Denington Estate
Wellingborough
Northamptonshire NN8 2RQ

INDEX